Discernment of Spirits in Marriage

Timothy M. Gallagher, OMV

Discernment of Spirits in Marriage

Ignatian Wisdom for Husbands and Wives

SOPHIA INSTITUTE PRESS
Manchester, New Hampshire

Imprimi potest: Very Reverend James A. Walther, O.M.V.,
Provincial, Province of St. Ignatius
Nihil obstat: Christopher P. Kelley, M.T.S., *Censor Librorum*

The nihil obstat and imprimi potest are declarations that a book or pamphlet is free of doctrinal or moral error and can be printed. No implication is contained therein that those who have granted the nihil obstat or imprimi potest agree with the contents, opinions or statements expressed.

Sophia Institute Press
Box 5284, Manchester, NH 03108
1-800-888-9344

www.SophiaInstitute.com

Sophia Institute Press® is a registered trademark of Sophia Institute.

Library of Congress Cataloging-in-Publication Data

Names: Gallagher, Timothy M., author.
Title: Discernment of spirits in marriage : Ignatian wisdom for husbands
and wives / Timothy M. Gallagher, OMV.
Description: Manchester, New Hampshire : Sophia Institute Press, 2020. |
Summary: "An application of St. Ignatius of Loyola's rules for the
discernment of spirits to the vocation of marriage"—Provided by
publisher.
Identifiers: LCCN 2020023103 | ISBN 9781644133477 (paperback) | ISBN
9781644133484 (ebook)
Subjects: LCSH: Married people—Religious life. | Marriage—Religious
life—Catholic Church. | Discernment of spirits. | Ignatius, of Loyola,
Saint, 1491-1556.
Classification: LCC BX2350.8 .G345 2020 | DDC 248.8/44—dc23
LC record available at https://lccn.loc.gov/2020023103

First printing

Contents

Appendices

Acknowledgments

I am deeply grateful to all who have helped me in the writing and publication of this book: to those who live the married vocation and who read the manuscript and offered invaluable advice, Elizabeth Valeri, Theresa Fagan, Anne Connors, Thomas and Hilda Gallagher, James and Margaret Gallagher, and Joan Marra; and to Charlie McKinney and Nora Malone of Sophia Institute Press for their warm and competent assistance in the publication of this book.

Introduction

This is a book about discernment of spirits in daily married life. For many of us, the term "discernment of spirits" is both inviting and mysterious. If asked to explain it, we might struggle a little.

What it means is this. We all know that as we live our spiritual lives, we experience ups and downs. At times, we feel God's closeness. Our prayer is alive. We find Mass engaging and participate willingly. Church activities are nourishing, and we look forward to them. Scripture speaks to our hearts and strengthens us for the day. We willingly take new steps to grow in our vocations.

But, if we are honest, we will also recognize that at other times, and for reasons we often do not understand, our spiritual energy seems to fade. We feel little inclination to pray, and when we do, our prayer is dry and difficult. At such times, we may pray less or be unhappy about the quality of our prayer. We find it harder to attend Mass during the week. Church activities no longer attract us in the same way. Those new steps for spiritual growth that seemed so inviting now appeal to us less, and we consider abandoning them....

These ups and downs go on constantly in our spiritual lives. Saint Ignatius of Loyola is not the only one who has described them, but no one else in our spiritual tradition has spoken of them with the clarity and practicality with which Saint Ignatius discusses them in his rules for the discernment of spirits. These fourteen rules, applied to the daily lives of husbands and wives, are the subject of this book.

For nearly forty years, I have studied, written, and taught these rules. I never planned this ministry! What caused it, under God's providence, was people's response to Saint Ignatius's teaching.

I have studied these rules in some depth, but it was not primarily study that revealed their richness. I discovered the power of these rules only when I began teaching them and found that people responded with excitement and enthusiasm. The rules helped them understand their spiritual experiences, those confusing alternations of energy and discouragement that we all undergo in the spiritual life. So often we experience these fluctuations without understanding them or knowing how to approach them. I found that Ignatius's rules gave people clarity and the tools they needed to respond to this experience.

Their desire for more led to a ministry focused specifically upon the rules. For decades now, I have seen the difference the rules make, how they *set captives free*, free from discouragement in the spiritual life and free to serve the God they love. This ministry has included religious, priests, and seminarians. Most of those, however, with whom I have shared these rules are laypeople.

A short, readable — I hope! — book that applies these rules to the lay vocation is long overdue. This book seeks to do that, with a specific focus on the married vocation. I believe, however, that readers who are single or in other vocations will find that it speaks to them as well. Ignatius's rules are universal: they apply to all, in all vocations.

Introduction

In this book, I employ the methodology I use when I present the rules and which is, to my mind, the most effective: a focus on Saint Ignatius's words and their illustration through examples. Each of the fourteen chapters corresponds to one of the fourteen rules. Each chapter contains two parts: experience and explanation. The chapter begins with a concrete experience in married life. The experience is then explained in the light of the corresponding rule.

These experiences are taken from the life of "Mark" and "Anne," who, by the second chapter, are married. Mark and Anne are not two concrete persons by that name: they are amalgams of the spiritual experiences of husbands and wives as they have shared this through these forty years. These examples might be called "reflected examples": they are real in that they reflect what occurs when married people live the spiritual life.

Mark and Anne's story is continuous from chapter to chapter, a kind of "semi-novel." The book's purpose is to portray the rules in daily married life and so aid readers to recognize and respond to this experience in their own lives.

This volume introduces the reader to the rules. Those who wish to pursue them further will find additional print and digital resources at the conclusion of this book.

For the convenience of the reader, I include the complete text of the rules in the appendices. In a first appendix, I provide my translation from the original Spanish of Saint Ignatius's text.[1] In this translation, I sacrifice literary elegance in order to reproduce

---

[1] In this appendix, I give Ignatius's text as he wrote it, with one exception: I have omitted the following from the title statement: "And these rules are more proper for the first week," which situates the rules in Ignatius's *Spiritual Exercises*.

the original text as closely as possible. I employ this translation in the chapters of this book. In a second appendix, I offer a freer rendering of Ignatius's text in language accessible for today.

From my earliest days of working with Saint Ignatius's rules, I have seen in them an expression of Jesus's mission as described in Luke 4: "The Spirit of the Lord is upon me.... He has sent me to proclaim liberty to captives and ... to let the oppressed go free" (v. 18). The purpose of these rules is to *set captives free*: to offer a path toward freedom to love and serve the Lord in daily life. May they guide spouses to that freedom and to the blessings that follow in their marriages and families.

1

A Loving Assault on the Heart

First Rule of Saint Ignatius

In persons who are going from mortal sin to mortal sin, the enemy is ordinarily accustomed to propose apparent pleasures to them, leading them to imagine sensual delights and pleasures in order to hold them more and make them grow in their vices and sins. In these persons the good spirit uses a contrary method, stinging and biting their consciences through their rational power of moral judgment.

"I never told you," Mark said, "how I saw you for the first time."

"You don't have to tell me," Anne replied, "I remember it well."

"I don't mean that day," Mark said. "I saw you once before then."

"You did?"

"Yes, and I want to tell you about it."

"I'd love to hear it. Let me ask: Why do you want to tell me today?"

"Because it's important to me that you know this now. We are talking about marriage, and we both want it. But before we take that step, I want you to know where I've been in the past. Then you can decide."

"You know how I feel about you. But yes, tell me. And thank you."

"Thank you?"

"Yes, for sharing about yourself in this way."

"I will," Mark said, "but it's not easy."

It was the afternoon of a fall day. Mark and Anne sat on a park bench, looking at the lake before them and the small island across the water. The sun shone upon the fall foliage.

Discernment of Spirits in Marriage

Distant sounds of traffic filtered through the air; where they sat, all was quiet.

∞

"I've told you about my family," Mark said, "but I've never said much about God. I know that's important to you, and so I want to tell you where I've been with God. I'm not proud of it. But it matters to me that you know, and that you know now before we make plans for the future.

"Overall, I had a good upbringing. It wasn't perfect, but my parents cared, and they tried. God was there in the family, not at the center, but he was a part of it. We went to Mass on Sundays, prayed before meals, and went to Confession once in a while. I had the usual catechism classes. I can't say that I applied myself much to any of this, but it was part of the family, and I accepted it." Anne listened in silence.

"In college," Mark continued, "I went to church, at least most of the time. But I started to get into habits that led me away. I think you can guess: partying, alcohol, some drugs, and some promiscuity. I did well academically, but this other side developed over those years.

"After I graduated, I started studies in optometry. They were demanding, and I wanted to do well, so I stopped some of this behavior. I didn't stop all of it, and it got so that I was going to church less and less." Anne continued to listen, gazing at the sun-flecked water before them.

"I finished the optometry program and did a year of residency. That's when I met Jim. He became my closest friend, and we spent a lot of time together. We would go out in the evenings after work and do things together on weekends. I liked Jim and enjoyed being with him, but it's clear to me now that he wasn't good for me. I still see him at work and sometimes outside of work.

"Until then, I'd been sort of half-and-half with God, not quite with him and not quite apart from him. Jim didn't have limits like this. When we were together, the kind of parties we'd go to got worse. There was more alcohol, more drugs, and more promiscuity. We went on vacation to the Caribbean, and I don't have to describe the things we did. It all felt exciting at the time. I don't know how I managed the residency with all of this going on, but somehow I did. After a while, I just stopped going to church." Anne gazed at Mark, listening intently.

Mark struggled to continue. "It was a strange life," he said. "Outwardly, I was a successful optometrist, preparing to begin my career. And I was having a lot of fun—at least, that's what Jim would've said and what I tried to say. But I was feeling more and more empty, more and more burdened. It got so that I hated to be alone. I always had to have the next thing to do, music to listen to, a screen to watch—anything so that I didn't have to feel the emptiness inside. I would be on the phone for hours, viewing things that were not good. My answer to the emptiness was to fill it with the same things that caused the emptiness. It didn't work."

Mark looked at Anne and said, "Anne, I don't know if I can describe this well: it was a kind of hell. It got so that I hated the way I was living, but I couldn't give it up. I'd say to myself, 'This is the last time I'll do this or that,' but then I'd do it again, and again, and again. And each time the darkness got darker." Anne nodded her understanding.

Mark paused, and then resumed. "One Saturday, I got back to my apartment late after a party of the worst kind, the kind in which really bad things happen. Jim and some others had invited me the day before, but I knew that I shouldn't go. Still, that evening I felt alone. As I did whenever I was feeling bad, I went on the phone and to the wrong websites. What I saw there awakened my interest in the party and led me to change my mind. I felt the pull: It would be fun. It would be great. This was living. Why hold back? What's the problem? I could have whatever I wanted. The pull got stronger, and I went.

"I got home at 2:00 a.m. I felt sick. I hated the apartment. I hated my life. I found painful questions arising: 'Why are you living this way? Why do you do it? You know it's a dead end. You know it's hurting you. You know you're destroying your future. Why do you keep doing what you know harms you? Why do you tell yourself that you're having fun when you know that it's not fun at all and that it's only causing you pain and emptiness? How dark does the darkness have to get before you'll change?'"

Mark broke off once more. For a minute he was silent, his face showing the heaviness of remembrance. Anne nodded her encouragement to continue.

With an effort, Mark did. "It was the worst pain I have ever felt. I knew that I couldn't go on like this, but I felt helpless to change. It was as if I was chained and couldn't get free. I knew that all options were on the table, and some of them were pretty frightening." Anne looked at Mark as he spoke, her whole focus on him and his words.

"Then a thought came to me: 'Why don't you pray? Why don't you ask God's help?' It stopped me. I hadn't prayed for years. I didn't even know if I could. What right did I have to turn to God for help when I'd abandoned him for so long? Why should he care?

"But somehow I did it. For the first time since I'd left home, I got down on my knees. It was a pretty broken and confused prayer.

It came down to this: 'God, I'm in pain. I'm ruining my life, and I can't change. *Please* do something, because I don't know what to do.' I stayed there, kneeling, for a long time.

"Then another thought came: 'This is Sunday. Why don't you go to Mass?' I had the same hesitation. I said to myself, 'You rejected God for years when things were going well, and now that you feel helpless you'll go to him? Why should he even want you?' But I didn't know what else to do. Finally, I decided that I'd go.

"I looked up the nearest parish, and it was Saint Joseph's. There was a noon Mass, and I went." Anne stirred. She began to see where this was leading.

"I sat in the back pew. The church was full. It was beautiful, and that was the first thing that hit me: it was so long since I'd experienced real beauty, not beauty to be selfishly exploited, but beauty that was clean and that lifted my heart.

"But it was the homily that really spoke to me. I've never forgotten it. The Gospel was the story of Zacchaeus [Luke 19:1–10]. The priest told how this man, whose life was so far from God, hoped only to glimpse Jesus from a distance, and how Jesus knew his need, set aside his journey and the other people, spent time with him, listened to him, talked with him, and changed his life. I knew the priest was speaking to me."

Mark looked again at Anne. "That was also the first time I saw you. You were a few rows in front of me. I saw you and how you prayed. I knew that God was real for you and that your faith meant a lot to you. I would have been embarrassed if you'd known that I was watching you pray, but I kept looking. And somehow, between the priest's words and your example, I decided that I would speak to the priest. After the Mass, I asked him if we could meet, and we set a time. We've met a number of times since."

Mark gave a brief, hesitant smile. "I also decided something else. I decided that I wanted to meet you. You know the rest of the story."

Mark stopped speaking. Anne, too, remained silent. The small sounds of the park and of the distant traffic again filled the air about them. Both looked at the sun's reflection on the water. A minute passed.

Then Anne reached out her hand and laid it on Mark's. "Thank you for trusting me enough to share that," she said. "And thank you for another reason too. You've seen my life in the Church, and it's true that I've tried to be faithful to God for some years now. But in my own way, I've experienced something of what you've just shared."

"You have?" Mark said with surprise.

"Yes. It was in college. For a few years I hardly went to Mass at all, and I started getting into the wrong things. But I was never happy. Then another student invited me to a retreat hosted by the campus Newman Center. I went, and I liked it. I liked the people, the conversation, all of it. It was so different from what I'd been experiencing. The retreat was a turning point, and from then on, things were different. That's why I say that I know the emptiness of that lifestyle. I also know, like you, the greater peace of living with God."

"Anne," Mark said, "It's my turn to say thank you, and more than I can say."

"Your years away from God," Anne said, "were real. But you turned away from them. That's real too. I've known you well for over two years now. I've seen how sincerely you try to live with God. And that's real. I've seen the goodness in you. That, too, is real."

Then Anne said, "I'm grateful for the way God has worked in your life, grateful that he brought us together, and grateful that I became part of your story that day. I'm so glad you've told me."

∞

In keeping with our methodology, at this point we will interrupt the story to review Mark's and Anne's experiences in the light of Ignatius's rules. During that difficult year and particularly on that troubled and grace-filled morning in his apartment, Mark experiences the workings of the good and bad spirits as Ignatius describes them in his first rule. He writes:

> The first rule: in persons who are going from mortal sin to mortal sin, the enemy is ordinarily accustomed to propose apparent pleasures to them, leading them to imagine sensual delights and pleasures in order to hold them more and make them grow in their vices and sins. In these persons the good spirit uses a contrary method, stinging and biting their consciences through their rational power of moral judgment.

These are persons far from God, living a life of serious sin. In such persons, Ignatius says, both the enemy and the good spirit will work. The *enemy*: Satan and his associated fallen angels; the wound of concupiscence we bear as a legacy of original sin; and all spiritually harmful influences around us in the world; the *good spirit*: God, the good angels, the power of grace given to us in Baptism, and all spiritually positive influences around us in the world—that is, God and all those influences that are from God and directed to God.

In such persons, Ignatius says, the enemy works in the imagination, filling it with images of "sensual delights and pleasures."

Discernment of Spirits in Marriage

The reason is evident: when the imagination is so filled, the person is likely to pursue the path of sin. Mark experiences this tactic of the enemy in college, optometry school, during his residency, and in striking fashion on that Saturday evening when he decides to go to the party: "That evening I felt alone. As I did whenever I was feeling bad, I went on the phone and to the wrong places. What I saw there awakened interest in the party and led me to change my mind. I felt the pull: It would be fun. It would be great. This was living. Why hold back? What's the problem? I could have whatever I wanted. The pull got stronger, and so I went."

In such persons, Ignatius continues, the good spirit does exactly the opposite, "stinging and biting their consciences." Through those years when he is far from God, Mark experiences this troubling action of the good spirit, a loving "stinging" and "biting" that calls him to make the one change that can ever give true happiness to the human heart. He feels this stinging and biting increasingly during his residency and with great force at 2:00 a.m. that Sunday morning: "Why are you living this way? Why do you do it? You know it's a dead end. You know it's hurting you. You know you're destroying your future. Why do you keep doing what you know harms you? Why do you tell yourself that you're having fun, when you know that it's not fun at all, and that it's only causing you pain and emptiness? How dark does the darkness have to get before you'll change?" This loving stinging and biting leads Mark back to Mass, to meet with the priest, to a new encounter with Jesus, and to a change of life — it leads him out of darkness and into light.

Anne, too, when she drifts away from the Lord in college, experiences this stinging and biting. Referring to that time, she tells Mark, "I was never happy." That unhappiness, the good spirit's stinging and biting, leads her, too, to turn to God and find peace.

If, at any time, you have experienced Mark's or Anne's situation, you now remember with deep gratitude the "stinging and biting" that brought you back to God. Ignatius's first rule also indicates that if any family members are far from God, God will never stop stinging and biting, never stop calling them back to himself. He loves them too much to simply let them go. Such knowledge awakens hope.

A final note. The images we allow into our imagination matter. What we do not allow to enter cannot harm us. A wise care to avoid harmful images and to absorb images of real beauty, holiness, and goodness, strengthens us enormously on the spiritual journey.

2

When You Want to Grow Closer to God

Second Rule of Saint Ignatius

In persons who are going on intensely purifying their sins and rising from good to better in the service of God our Lord, the method is contrary to that in the first rule. For then it is proper to the evil spirit to bite, sadden, and place obstacles, disquieting with false reasons, so that the person may not go forward. And it is proper to the good spirit to give courage and strength, consolations, tears, inspirations and quiet, easing and taking away all obstacles, so that the person may go forward in doing good.

∞

Mark parked the car and entered the house. He was returning from the noon Mass on Sunday. He found Anne in the kitchen with the three children. She had been to an earlier Mass.

They sat in the kitchen while the children, already fed, played. As they talked, Mark said, "Did you see that a Father Edward Reed is coming this Wednesday to give a talk? We had a priest by that name in the parish grade school I attended. From what the pastor said, it sounds like the same one. If it's the Father Reed I knew, I'd like to see him."

"I'll go with you," Anne replied. "Mom will be willing to babysit."

∞

On Wednesday evening, the church was full. Mark realized that others, too, knew and appreciated Father Reed. After an opening hymn, Father Reed walked to the pulpit. His steps were slow, and Mark saw that he had aged. His hair was white, his hands trembled a little, and he was thinner than Mark remembered him. He seemed tired.

But when he spoke, he was the Father Reed that Mark had known years before. A warmth emanated from him, a depth of

19

faith, a care for the people before him. He radiated the peace that arises from suffering and a long life of fidelity. The church grew quiet, absorbing his words. Time passed rapidly.

Father Reed finished his talk. The pastor stepped to the pulpit and thanked him. The choir led a final hymn, and people rose to leave. Anne, too, stood to go. Then she noticed that Mark had not moved. He sat, silent, immersed in thought. Anne resumed her place and waited a few minutes, respecting his silence.

Finally, she said, "Mark, what is it?"

Mark looked at her. "I always knew," he said slowly, "that God could be served. I've been trying to do that for some time. But I never knew, really knew, I mean, that God could be loved. I learned that from Father Reed this evening."

"What did you learn?" Anne asked.

"I think I've always been afraid of God. I've seen him as disappointed with me because of the way I've lived and how I struggle even now. When Father Reed spoke about the passage from Isaiah — 'You are precious in my sight, and honored, and I love you' [Isa. 43:4] — it wasn't even the words, though they are beautiful. It was the way he said them. You *knew* that this was real for him. He showed me that it's real for me too. It changes everything."

He rose, and together they left the church and returned home.

∞

After that, Anne noticed a change in Mark. Mass seemed to mean more to him, and he returned from church with more peace. One Sunday, the pastor invited his parishioners to spend ten minutes each day with the readings from the daily Mass. Mark was interested and spoke with Anne about this. She showed him how to find the readings, and he began this practice. Mark had never read the Bible on his own and did not always understand the text. But he strove to persevere.

A parishioner invited him to the men's prayer breakfast in the parish. Mark went and liked it. At 6:30 a.m. on the first Tuesday of each month, he joined the other men for breakfast, a talk, and discussion.

After a teaching on the sacrament of Reconciliation, Mark began to go to Confession more often. When he did, several things grew clearer. He saw that he had drifted into habits that were not good for him: certain ways of using the Internet, certain kinds of conversations, and some practices at work that skirted the unethical. Quietly, he changed his use of the Internet, distanced himself from those conversations, and eliminated those practices at work.

Anne noticed other changes. Mark became more patient, warmer, more sensitive to her needs and those of the children. He grew less self-centered and more available to others. He spent less time before the television, on the Internet, and with his friend Jim, and more time with the family. Their marriage felt stronger, and the children appeared happier. Something parallel happened at work, and Mark's colleagues appreciated his smile and his increased willingness to help.

In a new way, Mark found himself asking the Lord how to grow in his calling as a husband, father, office worker, and member of a parish. Each step on this path gave him energy to continue further on this path.

∞

At this point, Mark lives the spiritual situation that Ignatius describes in his second rule:

Discernment of Spirits in Marriage

> In persons who are going on intensely purifying their sins and rising from good to better in the service of God our Lord, the method is contrary to that in the first rule. For then it is proper to the evil spirit to bite, sadden, and place obstacles, disquieting with false reasons, so that the person may not go forward. And it is proper to the good spirit to give courage and strength, consolations, tears, inspirations and quiet, easing and taking away all obstacles, so that the person may go forward in doing good.

In this blessed spiritual situation, a person is growing both in freedom from sin ("persons who are going on intensely purifying their sins") and in the service of God ("rising from good to better in the service of God our Lord"). These two qualities are evident in Mark.

Mark identifies and seeks to remove his spiritually harmful habits: "Quietly, he changed his use of the Internet, distanced himself from those conversations, and eliminated those practices at work." At the same time, he becomes a more loving husband, father, and witness in the workplace: "Mark was growing more patient, warmer, more sensitive to her needs and those of the children.... Their marriage felt stronger and the children appeared happier. Something similar was happening at work." Mark perfectly fits the spiritual profile of rule 2.

When a person lives this grace-filled spiritual situation, how will the enemy work? And how will the good spirit work? This is the question Ignatius addresses in rule 2.

Ignatius is now speaking directly to you. Yes, we all have weaknesses and imperfections. But if you are reading this, it is because you sincerely desire to overcome sin and to love God. From rule 2 on, therefore, you will find nothing abstract in Ignatius's teaching.

∞

First e-mail from Jim to Mark, Monday morning:

> *Hi, Mark. I haven't seen you in a few weeks. Where've you been? It's time we got together. A group of us are going to Chet's Place this Saturday evening. Do you want to join us?*

First e-mail from Mark to Jim, a half hour later:

> *Hi, Jim. Good to hear from you. Things have gotten busy recently, and I haven't been out much. Thanks for the invitation for Saturday, but I won't be able to make it. Let's look for another time.*

Second e-mail from Jim to Mark, an hour later:

> *You never have time to get together these days. What's up?*

Second e-mail from Mark to Jim, three hours later:

> *Things have gotten busy, that's all. Some new commitments.*

Third e-mail from Jim to Mark, ten minutes later:

> *Is it all this new business with the Church?*

Discernment of Spirits in Marriage

Third e-mail from Mark to Jim, two hours later, in the afternoon:

Yes, since you ask, that's part of it. If you want, we can talk about it sometime.

Fourth e-mail from Jim to Mark, five minutes later:

What's come over you? Have you got something against us and Chet's Place?

Fourth e-mail from Mark to Jim, a half hour later:

I'd rather not talk about it by e-mail. As I said, I'll talk about it, if you want, sometime when we meet.

Fifth e-mail from Jim to Mark, one minute later:

Mark, I know you. You get these enthusiasms, but they never last. You think you're going to change in some way, but it will end pretty quickly. Remember, I know who you are and what you've done. Make your efforts, if you want. Try if you like. But you know, and I know, that it's not going to last. Don't tell me that you haven't been thinking the same thing yourself. You can let me know when you're ready to meet in the usual way. That's it for today. Have a good evening—if your busyness allows it.

∞

That evening:

When Mark returned from work, Anne immediately saw that he was discouraged. After the children were in bed, he spoke with her. He told Anne about Jim, about the invitation to join the group at Chet's Place, the e-mails, and how they ended.

"I'm trying to resist Jim's words," Mark said, "but they touch a vulnerable spot, and it isn't easy. His words discourage me because there's a deep place in me that thinks the same, that this is all too good to be true, that a few months can't really change what I've been for years. Jim has just put into words what I've been thinking myself all along. And it hits home in a deeper way when someone who knows you well says it to you.

"I don't know what's happening," Mark continued. "I'd been feeling happy about my relationship with God, more than in years. But even before I got Jim's e-mails, that peace was less, and sometimes it feels like it's gone completely. I just don't have the same happiness. I don't know: sometimes I feel heavy, a kind of sadness about all this struggling and striving to change."

Mark looked at Anne. "I can't help thinking," he said, "that Jim is right. How long can I keep up this prayer, this going to church, this effort to make better friends and avoid evenings like Chet's Place on Saturday? None of this has lasted in the past. I can't argue with Jim. It's true. I get these enthusiasms. I try. But it never lasts. It's probably going to happen again. I don't think I'll ever really change.'

Anne had heard Mark talk like this before, but this seemed more serious. His next words took her completely by surprise.

Discernment of Spirits in Marriage

"Maybe I'm just trying to impress you," he said. "Maybe I just want, for the first time, some respect from your family. They never thought I was good enough for you, and they didn't like how I'd been away from the Church. Maybe that's what this is really about. Maybe it's all self-centered. Maybe I'm competing with you so that the children will think better of me. Maybe I have to stop fooling myself and accept that I am who I am, and that I'll never be different."

∞

This evening, Mark experiences the classic tactics of the enemy in one who is progressing spiritually. Ignatius writes that in such persons, "it is proper to the evil spirit to *bite, sadden,* and *place obstacles, disquieting with false reasons,* so that the person may not go forward." Four tactics. When you try to grow spiritually, you, too, will experience them. To be aware of these tactics, name them, and reject them is key for continued progress in the spiritual life.

As Mark's experience indicates, there is nothing dramatic about these tactics: this is ordinary experience in the daily spiritual life — which is why it is so important to recognize and reject it. Most of the spiritual life is lived precisely on this ordinary, daily level. In Mark's case, much depends on whether he believes these discouraging lies of the enemy and abandons his efforts to grow, or whether he identifies and rejects these tactics. The same, with our individual nuances, is true in our spiritual lives as well.

- The enemy *bites,* that is, gnaws at, seeks to diminish, the peace that spiritual growth has brought the person. Mark tells Anne that his "peace was less, and sometimes it feels like it's gone completely." Such "biting" is an effective tactic if we are not aware of it. From this to "What's the point of all these efforts if I don't even feel happy anymore?" is a small step. But if Mark recognizes, and we recognize, this biting as a tactic of the "liar and the father of lies" (John 8:44) and we reject it, it will not harm us.

• The enemy *saddens*, that is, seeks to diminish the joy of new closeness to God, to insinuate that this path is hard and heavy and will remain so. Mark tells Anne, "Sometimes I feel heavy, a kind of sadness about all this struggling and striving to change." The comments just made about the enemy's biting apply equally here: our need is to recognize this tactic and reject it.

• This evening, the enemy attempts to *place obstacles* in Mark's path. Mark tells Anne, "How long can I keep up this prayer, this going to church, this effort to make better friends and avoid evenings like Chet's Place on Saturday? None of this has lasted in the past." To the one growing, the enemy insinuates: "It's too hard. You're too weak. You can't keep this up. You are doomed to fail. You'll never change." Obstacles, obstacles, obstacles. We have all heard this voice when we've wanted to grow.

There is no shame in experiencing these tactics of the enemy! I repeat this because of its importance: there is no shame in experiencing these tactics of the enemy. We all do. This is ordinary spiritual experience. What matters is to recognize these discouraging lies for the tactics of the enemy that they are and reject them, so that they will never harm us.

Discernment of Spirits in Marriage

• Finally, the enemy will attempt to *disquiet with false reasons*. Mark tells Anne, "Maybe I'm just trying to impress you. Maybe I just want, for the first time, some respect from your family." No! None of this was present that night Mark heard Father Reed speak, nor in the efforts that followed. Now the enemy is attempting to trouble Mark with deceptive considerations about what "really" underlies his efforts to grow spiritually: this is all self-centered. Once more, if Mark believes these lies, they will weaken his spiritual energy; if he identifies them for the lies they are, they will not harm him. This is discernment in daily life.

∞

From Anne's diary, Monday, a week later:

I worried about Mark after we spoke a week ago: he was so discouraged. For the first time, I was afraid he might give up his new life of faith. It's been such a blessing for our marriage and our family. I wish he would just stop speaking with Jim.

I prayed about it and then had a thought: Why shouldn't Mark speak with Father Reed? He likes Father and respects his wisdom. I mentioned it to Mark. He didn't say anything, but I could see that the idea struck him.

On Friday, he told me that he had called Father Reed, and they had agreed to meet Sunday afternoon. Today he told me about their meeting.

It seems that Father Reed is quite ill. He has multiple system atrophy and will live, at most, another seven to nine years, most likely less. That explains the slowness of

*movement we saw in the church, the tremors, and the effort
to speak. Mark finds something deeply holy in him and a
great wisdom. From Mark's description of their meeting, it
seems that he is right.*

∞

That Sunday afternoon, Mark arrived at the rectory and rang
the doorbell. Slow steps approached from within, and Father
Reed opened the door. He smiled a greeting, and they moved to
the front sitting room. Sun streamed through the open venetian
blinds, and the occasional sounds of cars passing by could be
heard. Mark introduced himself, and they shared memories of
earlier school days.

After a brief prayer, Father Reed settled himself to listen.
Mark explained why he had come. He spoke of his life of faith
in recent years and his present discouragement. Father Reed
listened attentively, occasionally nodding his understanding.

When Mark had finished, Father Reed thought for a moment
and said, "Mark, what has given you strength in your new life
of faith?"

Mark considered briefly, and answered, "It started because I
was so unhappy about the way I was living before. Then, getting
to know Anne and seeing her life of faith was a great encouragement. Your talk also helped. You showed me that I could
love God and not just serve him from a distance. That gave
me energy and made me want more. The things I started doing
also made a difference: meeting the other men at the prayer
breakfast, the talks, going to Confession, getting to daily Mass
when I could, and trying to pray with the Bible, even though
I'm not very good at it. Anne has been an encouragement every
step of the way."

"You have many sources of strength," Father Reed replied, "and it's good to hear of them."

"Yes, they've made a real difference. I'm grateful for them."

Father Reed reflected and then asked, "What has relating to God been like as all this has been happening?"

"It has felt," Mark answered, "like God is getting closer, more real. Sometimes I feel a peace, a rightness about my life. I can't describe it well, but I feel it, and it makes everything worthwhile. Sometimes it even moves me to tears, if that makes sense."

Father Reed nodded, "Yes, that makes a lot of sense." He continued, "You've mentioned a number of helpful spiritual practices. Tell me, how did you start doing them?"

"Well, that first Sunday Mass because I was desperate and knew that I needed to do something. It was the only thing I could think of. Confession because I felt such peace after I went the first time. I thought that if one Confession helped this way, what would happen if I kept going? The prayer breakfast because one of the men invited me, and I wanted to meet others with the same interest in spiritual things. The Bible because the priest suggested it at Mass."

Father Reed smiled, "Well, God certainly seems to have been active!" Then he asked, "As you've been doing these things, what has happened in your life?"

"I've gotten happier," Mark replied, "and I find that these practices get easier as I continue them. I grow more confident that, with God's help, I really can change and persevere. It matters to me because I know it makes Anne happy. Our marriage is becoming stronger, and our family is more united. When I'm doing these things, I feel like God will see me through."

"Then you had the e-mails with Jim, and that discouraged you."

"Yes. It seemed so real, because sometimes, even before Jim said anything, I felt like I couldn't persevere and that I'd go back to the way things were before. I'd been discouraged at times, but after Jim wrote, things got really dark, and I was losing hope."

"How do you feel now about what Jim wrote?"

Mark smiled briefly. "Well, after what I've just said to you, it seems clear that I should forget what he wrote and keep focused on what God is doing."

Father Reed nodded agreement and said, "Yes, I'd say that's just what you should do."

∞

On this Sunday afternoon, with Father Reed's help, Mark names the tactics of the good spirit in one who is rising toward God. Ignatius writes that in such persons, "It is proper to the good spirit to give *courage and strength, consolations, tears, inspirations and quiet, easing and taking away all obstacles*, so that the person may go forward in doing good." Five grace-filled tactics. When we seek to grow spiritually, we will experience them. Welcome them! Drink in their strength! They sustain us on the journey.

• The good spirit gives *courage and strength*, that is, provides encouragement, energy, and vitality on the path of growth. Mark experiences this action of the good spirit through Anne's witness and accompaniment, Father Reed's talk, regular Confession, Mass during the week, the support of the men at the prayer breakfast, and the Bible.

How has the good spirit given you courage and strength to grow spiritually? Can you name the ways? Through which persons? Which encounters? What words? What times of prayer? Of sharing with others?

Discernment of Spirits in Marriage

Here the call is to recognize the action of the good spirit, to receive it, and to allow God to provide us with courage and strength for the journey.

• The good spirit gives *consolations*, that is, times when our hearts grow warm with a sense of God's love and closeness. Mark tells Father Reed, "Sometimes I feel a peace, a rightness about my life. I can't describe it well, but I feel it, and it makes everything worthwhile." Such consolations are a blessed gift to hearten us on the way. We have all experienced consolations, and we are rightly grateful for these gifts. Do not hesitate to open your heart to them when God gives them. Allow God to love and strengthen you through them.

• The good spirit gives *tears*, that is, a physical sharing in the consolation of the heart. Mark tells Father Reed, "Sometimes it even moves me to tears, if that makes sense." As Father Reed replies, it does. We all remember tears of this kind, and we rightly treasure them for the spiritual strength they give.

• The good spirit gives *inspirations*, that is, moments of clarity, times when we see the next step, when the doubt is resolved, when we know where the Lord is leading and what we need to do. Father Reed asks Mark how he began his new steps in the spiritual life, and Mark names various inspirations of the good spirit: Mass, through an interior prompting; Confession, because it helped so greatly and he wanted more of such grace; the prayer breakfast, because one of the men invited him, and the like. Through awakening thoughts and desires in Mark's own heart, and through others, the good spirit gives inspirations that point the way forward.

• The good spirit *eases and takes away all obstacles*, that is, reveals that perseverance and progress are possible, that the obstacles the enemy places in our path can be overcome. Mark tells Father Reed, "I grow more confident that, with God's help, I really can change and persevere.... I feel like God will see me through." His words reveal the blessed action of the good spirit, easing the path and removing all obstacles.

Four tactics of the enemy: *to bite, sadden, place obstacles, and disquiet with false reasons.* Five tactics of the good spirit: *to give courage and strength, consolations, tears, inspirations, and ease all obstacles.* If we learn these well, watch for them, identify them, and reject the first and embrace the second, we will, as Ignatius says, "go forward" on the path of growth.

3

Grace in a Time of Anxiety

Third Rule of Saint Ignatius

The third is of spiritual consolation. I call it consolation when some interior movement is caused in the soul, through which the soul comes to be inflamed with love of its Creator and Lord, and, consequently when it can love no created thing on the face of the earth in itself, but only in the Creator of them all. Likewise when it sheds tears that move to love of its Lord, whether out of sorrow for one's sins, or for the passion of Christ our Lord, or because of other things directly ordered to his service and praise. Finally, I call consolation every increase of hope, faith, and charity, and all interior joy that calls and attracts to heavenly things and to the salvation of one's soul, quieting it and giving it peace in its Creator and Lord.

∞

From Anne's diary, Wednesday, two weeks later:

I continue to worry about Mark. Things were better after he met with Father Reed, but it didn't last. He seems discouraged again and on edge. I don't know what to do. He won't talk about it anymore and gets angry if I try.

From Anne's diary, Friday, two days later:

Mark has stopped praying with the readings in the morning. He continues to block my attempts to talk about what's happening.

From Anne's diary, Tuesday, four days later:

I don't think Mark went to the prayer breakfast today. If not, it's the first one he's missed since he began going. He seems to be growing more and more discouraged. Jim is a bad influence, and they've seen more of each other recently. I tried to suggest that he speak again with Father Reed, but Mark didn't reply. Am I at fault somehow?

*What should I do? I worry, and I don't know how to
help. I'm afraid the children will sense the tension. They
probably already have.*

From Anne's diary, Thursday, two days later:

*Mark is spending more and more time with Jim. It's not
good.*

From Anne's diary, Saturday, two days later:

*Today I remembered something. The last time there was
tension between Mark and me, it was about moving.
There were reasons for a move, and he wanted to talk
about it. With increasing traffic, his commute was getting
longer. As each child was born, the house was getting more
crowded. The place he wanted to move to was closer to his
parents. I didn't even want to talk about it. I felt like taking care of the children and getting the day's work done was
all I could handle. And I'd come to like the area and the
neighbors. I didn't want to move. Just talking about it felt
like too much. So there was a tension between us.*

*One morning, I dropped the children off at school and
walked over to the Adoration chapel. The monstrance was
on the altar just in front of me. I sat, looking at it. In that
moment, I felt Jesus's presence there before me and a deep
sense of being loved. For a few minutes, that was all I felt:
Jesus's real presence and his warm love for me. In that moment, too, something resistant in me gave way. I knew that
I needed to let Mark talk about the move, and I knew that I*

was ready to do it. We spoke that evening, and the tension began to wane.

Monday, after I drop the children off, I'll go to the Adoration chapel.

On Monday morning, when the children were in school, Anne crossed the parking lot to the Adoration chapel. She entered. One woman was there, praying silently. Anne walked to the front pew, genuflected, and sat, gazing at the monstrance on the altar.

For a time, she thought of nothing in particular. She simply looked at the Blessed Sacrament and allowed her heart to settle. Then she began to pray Psalm 23, a text she knew by heart and loved. She said the first words, "The LORD is my shepherd; there is nothing I shall want," and could go no further. A warm sense of Jesus's presence there before her on the altar, arose in her heart. A surety of his closeness, of his knowledge of her need, and of his love for her welled up within. A sense of safety awakened, an assurance that he would guide her and Mark through their present struggles. Slowly she repeated the words, "The LORD is my shepherd; there is nothing I shall want."

Tears came, tears that lightened the anxiety she had carried for weeks, tears that expressed her certainty that Jesus was with her. She felt a new hope and a confidence that Jesus would assist them through this difficult time, that he would help her do her part. His presence before her was alive and real. She *knew* that she was not alone. Again healing tears flowed. Warmed by the gift given her, she felt loved, ready to love Mark and to walk with him through his trial.

Time passed in silence. Anne sat without moving, her heart at peace. Then, slowly, she prayed the remainder of the psalm.

When she finished, she rose, returned to the car, and drove home.

∞

That Monday morning, as she sits in the chapel, Anne experiences the spiritual consolation that Ignatius describes in his third rule:

> The third is of spiritual consolation. I call it consolation when some interior movement is caused in the soul, through which the soul comes to be inflamed with love of its Creator and Lord, and, consequently when it can love no created thing on the face of the earth in itself, but only in the Creator of them all. Likewise when it sheds tears that move to love of its Lord, whether out of sorrow for one's sins, or for the passion of Christ our Lord, or because of other things directly ordered to his service and praise. Finally, I call consolation every increase of hope, faith, and charity, and all interior joy that calls and attracts to heavenly things and to the salvation of one's soul, quieting it and giving it peace in its Creator and Lord.

"The third is of *spiritual consolation*." Two words: "consolation" and "spiritual." *Consolation* is an uplifting movement of the heart (joy, love, gratitude, hope, peace, and similar stirrings), and Ignatius specifies that this uplifting movement of the heart occurs on the *spiritual* level, the level of faith and of our relationship with God. This spiritual level is apparent in Anne's experience that Monday morning in the chapel: it is Jesus's presence in the

Blessed Sacrament, his love, and his assurance of help that give Anne joy, hope, and peace. She experiences *consolation* on the specifically *spiritual* level. It is of such spiritual consolation that Ignatius speaks in rule 3.

In her prayer before the Blessed Sacrament, Anne experiences the different forms of spiritual consolation that Ignatius describes in rule 3:

- As she prays this Monday morning, a warm sense of Jesus's love for her stirs in Anne's heart ("the soul comes to be inflamed with love of its Creator and Lord").

- A second experience of spiritual consolation is more evident in Anne's earlier time of prayer in the chapel, as narrated in her journal. When, Ignatius says, the heart is inflamed, warmed, enkindled in this way, attachments that hinder our openness to God's leading in our lives may dissolve ("and, consequently when it can love no created thing on the face of the earth in itself, but only in the Creator of them all"). Anne writes, "That was all that I felt: Jesus's real presence and his warm love for me. In that moment, too, something resistant in me gave way."

- When Anne prays this Monday morning, healing tears come to her eyes ("when it sheds tears that move to love of its Lord, whether out of sorrow for one's sins, or for the passion of Christ our Lord, or because of other things directly ordered to his service and praise").

- As she prays, Anne feels a new assurance that Jesus will be with her and Mark in this difficult time ("increase of hope").

- Sitting in prayer before the Blessed Sacrament, a lively awareness of Jesus's real presence in the Eucharist stirs in Anne's heart ("increase of faith").

- In her prayer, a deep sense of Jesus's love for her and a strengthened ability to love Mark awaken in Anne ("increase of charity").

- A blessed joy fills Anne's heart during her prayer ("all interior joy that calls and attracts to heavenly things and to the salvation of one's soul").

All of us have experienced times of spiritual consolation, and we rightly thank God for them. A glance at our past will bring to mind such experiences and how they blessed us on our spiritual path.

When God gives spiritual consolation, open your heart to receive the love and strength he imparts through this gift. Spiritual consolation is an affective language through which God, in his love, speaks to our hearts and sustains us on the way.

4

An Evening in Darkness

Fourth Rule of Saint Ignatius

The fourth is of spiritual desolation. I call desolation all the contrary of the third rule, such as darkness of soul, disturbance in it, movement to low and earthly things, disquiet from various agitations and temptations, moving to lack of confidence, without hope, without love, finding oneself totally slothful, tepid, sad, and as if separated from one's Creator and Lord. For just as consolation is contrary to desolation, in the same way the thoughts that come from consolation are contrary to the thoughts that come from desolation.

∞

From Mark's journal, Saturday, six weeks later:

Things are a mess, and I have to do something about this.

Some months ago, John, whom I met at the prayer breakfast, told me that in AA they were encouraged to keep a journal. He said it helped. I know Anne does it. I never have, but maybe it can help me now. So I'm trying it.

Talking with Father Reed was good, but it didn't last. The past month or so has been dark, and I know Anne feels it. She wants me to talk about it, but I'm too ashamed, and I keep her at a distance. The old habits have returned, and the new ones have disappeared. I haven't been to the prayer breakfast in two months. I haven't gone to Mass during the week in three weeks, and I've stopped praying with the Scripture readings. I've been seeing more of Jim and the group, and that moves me in a bad direction. I know it's not good, but I don't seem able to stop.

Discernment of Spirits in Marriage

*What is the answer? Where do I turn? Next Tuesday
is the first Tuesday of the month and the prayer breakfast.
Maybe I should go.*

From Mark's journal, next Tuesday evening, shortly after
supper:

*I went to the prayer breakfast today, and it felt good. The
men were glad to see me. The talk was on prayer, and it
helped. Just being there with the others at breakfast and then
hearing the talk lifted a part of the darkness I've been feeling. I stayed for Mass with some of the others, and that was
welcome too. I'd almost forgotten that sense of peace and
rightness. During the Mass, God felt closer, and I felt more
hope that something could change.*

*I stayed for a few minutes after Mass, grateful for
the prayer breakfast and the Mass. I decided that in the
evening, I would get the booklet with the daily readings,
prepare to start the prayer again, and begin the next
morning.*

*Today work was tiring. I never stopped from the mo-
ment I arrived until I left for home. I had to tell two elderly
patients that they would probably lose their sight. You try
not to let it affect you, but it's never easy when you see
how sad they become. One man's wife was with him, and
she cried. The other lives alone and doesn't know how he'll
manage. Then another patient got angry when I explained
her situation, and she told me she was going to change
optometrists.*

*At supper, things were tense. I was tired, and the
discouragement had returned. Anne sensed it, and maybe*

the children too. I left the table as soon as I decently could. I know Anne is suffering.

∞

It was ten o'clock that same evening, and Mark was alone in his study. Anne and the children were asleep. He had just finished his preparations for work the next day.

Mark sat at his desk for a moment without moving. Then he remembered his decision that morning to take the booklet with the readings and prepare to pray the next day. But the morning's energy and hope were no longer present. Mark felt no sense of God's closeness and love. Everything seemed heavy and dark. He was troubled and discouraged. Familiar voices sounded within: "You'll never do it. You'll try to change, but you'll always fail. You will this time too. This morning didn't change anything. You're still you. You want to try praying with the readings again? How long did it last before? It won't last any longer this time. Why do you keep making these useless efforts?"

Mark sat with both hands before him on his desk. A few inches in front of one hand was the booklet with the readings. Nothing in him wanted to reach out for it. He looked at it and felt no desire to take it up, no willingness to open it.

A few inches in front of the other hand was the phone. Everything in Mark wanted to reach for it. He knew that when he felt this way and turned to the phone, one touch could become fifty, could become two hundred. As the touches mounted, the content he viewed would spiral downward. But the desire was there, and it was strong. Mark felt too weak, too discouraged, too burdened to resist it.

Discernment of Spirits in Marriage

∞

This Tuesday evening, in the silence of his study, Mark experiences the spiritual desolation that Ignatius describes in his fourth rule:

> The fourth is of spiritual desolation. I call desolation all the contrary of the third rule, such as darkness of soul, disturbance in it, movement to low and earthly things, disquiet from various agitations and temptations, moving to lack of confidence, without hope, without love, finding oneself totally slothful, tepid, sad, and as if separated from one's Creator and Lord. For just as consolation is contrary to desolation, in the same way the thoughts that come from consolation are contrary to the thoughts that come from desolation.

"The fourth is of *spiritual desolation*." Two words: "desolation" and "spiritual." *Desolation* is a heavy movement of the heart (sadness, discouragement, hopelessness, anxiety, and similar stirrings), and Ignatius specifies that this heavy movement of the heart occurs on the *spiritual* level, on the level of faith and of our relationship with God. The spiritual level is apparent in Mark's experience this evening in his study: the heaviness and discouragement he feels are very much in relationship to God, prayer, and his spiritual life. Mark experiences *desolation* on the specifically *spiritual* level. It is of such spiritual desolation that Ignatius speaks in rule 4.

Sitting in his study, Mark undergoes the different forms of spiritual desolation that Ignatius describes in rule 4:

- This evening, everything feels heavy and dark ("darkness of soul").

- Anxiety troubles his heart ("disturbance in the soul").

- He inclines toward the phone in a harmful way ("movement to low and earthly things").

- He has lost his peace and is subject to temptation ("disquiet from various agitations and temptations").

- The old voices resound: "You'll never change" ("moving to lack of confidence").

- And further: "What's the point of making another effort? It won't last" ("without hope").

- He does not feel God's warm and loving presence ("without love").

- He has no energy for prayer ("finding oneself totally slothful").

- He feels no inclination for spiritual things ("totally tepid").

- He experiences no joy ("totally sad").

- He feels utterly alone, as though God were far away ("as if separated from one's Creator and Lord").

Again, there is *no shame* in experiencing such spiritual desolation: this is simply what happens when we live the spiritual life in a fallen, redeemed, and loved world. What does matter is to be aware of this experience, to name it for the tactic of the enemy that it is — the discouraging lie of spiritual desolation — and firmly to reject it.

Discernment of Spirits in Marriage

A question. What if Mark is *not* aware of this experience, does not understand it for the tactic of the enemy that it is, and does not reject it? What if he does reach out for the phone and sets it down two hundred touches later? What will be in his heart when he retires that evening? What will be in his heart when he rises the next morning and prepares for the day?

But *what if*, by God's grace and with some courage, Mark does become aware of this experience, understands it for the discouraging lie of the enemy that it is, and *reaches out for the booklet* with the readings, never touching the phone that evening? Now what will be in his heart when he retires? What will be in his heart when he rises the next morning and prepares for the day?

The consequences in either case are significant. Let us suppose that Mark reaches out for the phone. What will his prayer look like the next morning? A week later? A month? A year? Five years? What impact will this diminishment of his prayer have on his marriage? On his role as a father? As a member of the Church? As a witness to Christ in the workplace?

Let us suppose, however, that Mark reaches out for the booklet. Now what will his prayer look like the next morning? A week later? A month? A year? Five years? What impact will this growth in prayer have on his marriage? On his role as a father? As a member of the Church? As a witness to Christ in the workplace?

Clearly, it matters that we recognize and reject spiritual desolation. It matters all the more because the greatest part of the spiritual life occurs on this daily level. The growth or diminishment of our spiritual lives is largely determined by these many, "small" daily decisions. It is precisely on this daily level that Ignatius wants to assist us. He does so by clarifying the tactics of the enemy and then showing us how to reject them. His remaining ten rules will be dedicated to this purpose.

I believe that for most dedicated people, for most of the way on the spiritual journey, spiritual desolation is the main obstacle: the times when we grow discouraged, lose energy for spiritual things, and incline to regress spiritually in various ways. I believe, therefore, that Ignatius's teaching on spiritual desolation, a teaching that equips us to be aware of it, name it, and reject it, is among the greatest gifts he gives us for our daily spiritual lives. The experience of many confirms this.

Can we envision a spiritual life that is growing in freedom from spiritual desolation? Can we conceive the joy, the hope, and the fruitfulness of such a life? Of a marriage lived in such freedom? A family? A presence in the Church and in the world? For many years I have seen these rules provide clarity and hope to people of faith.

∞

A final sentence in rule 4 links it with rule 3: "For just as consolation is contrary to desolation, in the same way the thoughts that come from consolation are contrary to the thoughts that come from desolation." Spiritual consolation and spiritual desolation are movements of the heart directly contrary to each other: *spiritual consolation* is an uplifting movement of the heart (joy, peace, gratitude, and similar stirrings); *spiritual desolation* is a heavy movement of the heart (sadness, anxiety, discouragement, and similar stirrings).

Ignatius notes that when the *heart* experiences the uplift of spiritual consolation or the heaviness of spiritual desolation, something corresponding happens in the *head*: thoughts arise from the one space of the heart and the other, and these, too, are contrary. Thus, when Mark attends the prayer breakfast that Tuesday and stays for Mass, his heart experiences God's closeness and a new hope (spiritual consolation). In his spiritual consolation, thoughts arise: "It is time to resume my prayer with the readings. I will look at the booklet this evening, prepare, and start again tomorrow morning." When he sits at his desk that evening, feeling far from God, without energy for spiritual things, and without hope (spiritual desolation), other thoughts arise: "Why try to start the prayer again? It's not going to last. It's just useless effort."

As is evident, the thoughts that arise in time of *spiritual desolation* are exactly the contrary of the thoughts that arise in *spiritual consolation*. Throughout this set of rules, the conclusion is clear: Accept the thoughts that arise in spiritual consolation! Reject the thoughts that arise in spiritual desolation!

We can also see the importance of living the discerning life, of knowing when we are in spiritual consolation or spiritual desolation. The meaning of much that stirs within clarifies when we do. Through the discerning life, we are set free from harm and set free to grow in the vocation that God has given us.

5

What You Should Never Do

Fifth Rule of Saint Ignatius

In time of desolation never make a change, but be firm and constant in the proposals and determination in which one was the day preceding such desolation, or in the determination in which one was in the preceding consolation. Because, as in consolation the good spirit guides and counsels us more, so in desolation the bad spirit, with whose counsels we cannot find the way to a right decision.

∞

From Mark's journal, Tuesday, a week later:

The struggle continues. Prayer is hit-or-miss, and some-
times I make wrong choices. Still too much of Jim and
all that goes with this. Were those months of the prayer
breakfast, Mass during the week, and daily prayer just a
brief exception from who I really am?

From Mark's journal, Thursday, two days later:

Some weeks ago, Anne suggested that I speak with Fa-
ther Reed. Maybe she was right.

From Mark's journal, Wednesday, the following week:

I called Father Reed, and we agreed to meet Saturday
afternoon next week. He has several doctor appoint-
ments in the intervening days: it seems things have
recently worsened for him. Even so, after we spoke, I
felt my heart lift. It will be good to talk with him about
all this.

Discernment of Spirits in Marriage

From Anne's journal, Friday, two days later:

*Mark still won't talk about it, but I see that the struggle
continues. I had such hope for our marriage in recent
months. Now it's harder to hope.*

*After that Monday in the chapel, I decided that I
would stop there every Monday morning after dropping
off the children. I've been doing that, and it always helps.
I'll stop in next Monday as well.*

From Mark's journal, the same Friday:

*Another tough day at work, a day without prayer,
and with a few things that were not good. I can see the
discouragement in Anne as this continues. I find myself
rethinking next Saturday's meeting with Father Reed.
I've already spoken with him once. It was nice, but it
didn't last. Why should it be any different this time?*

From Anne's journal, Saturday, one day later:

*I keep trying, and I keep praying, but nothing seems to
change. Maybe those visits to the Adoration chapel are
more about nice feelings than anything substantial. In
any case, they don't seem to have changed things.*

From Mark's journal, Sunday, one day later:

*Today was not good. I went to Mass, but I began feeling
again like I don't belong. I was short with Anne and the
children, and things got a little heavy. All the old patterns*

*are alive today, and they draw me. More and more I feel
that there's no point in talking with Father Reed. He'll
be nice about it, he always is, but he'll wish that I would
improve after meeting with him. Very likely, he, too, will
figure that there isn't much point in meeting. Maybe I
should call and tell him that I can't make it on Saturday.*

From Anne's journal, Sunday, the same day:

*This was our worst day yet. I could see that Mark barely
wanted to go to Mass. He was tense all day, and so was
I. The children felt it and got uneasy. I try not to get discouraged, but today I am feeling disheartened. I try, and
I try, and nothing seems to change. Things even seem to
get worse. The way I feel tonight, I don't want to go to
the chapel tomorrow morning. There seems no point. I'm
tired of trying.*

∞

On this Sunday, both Mark and Anne will benefit greatly from
Ignatius's fifth rule:

In time of desolation never make a change, but be firm
and constant in the proposals and determination in
which one was the day preceding such desolation, or in
the determination in which one was in the preceding
consolation. Because, as in consolation the good spirit
guides and counsels us more, so in desolation the bad
spirit, with whose counsels we cannot find the way
to a right decision.

Discernment of Spirits in Marriage

In his first sentence, Ignatius provides the norm: "In time of desolation never make a change." Eight words that have blessed disciples of Jesus for five hundred years: in time of desolation never make a change! *In time of desolation* — when you know you are experiencing the heaviness of spiritual desolation — *never make a change* — never change anything in your spiritual life that you had planned before that spiritual desolation began.

On this Sunday, both Mark and Anne experience the discouragement of spiritual desolation. In their time of desolation, both consider changing a spiritual proposal they had in place before the desolation began: Mark, to speak with Father Reed on Saturday, and Anne, to pray in the Adoration chapel on Monday morning. Their experience is precisely that envisaged by Ignatius in rule 5.

His counsel is clear: in time of spiritual desolation, *never* change any spiritual proposal that you had in place before that desolation began. If Mark knows rule 5, then he knows that he should meet with Father Reed on Saturday as he planned before the desolation began. If Anne knows rule 5, then she knows that she should go to the Adoration chapel on Monday morning as she planned before the desolation began. Very likely, that meeting with Father Reed and that prayer in the chapel will help significantly to overcome the desolation. For good reason the enemy attacks our spiritual proposals in time of desolation! And for good reason Ignatius counsels us never to make such changes!

Ignatius learns from experience that the enemy will generally attack our spiritual proposals — to pray at a certain time this day, to go on that retreat next month, to assist at daily Mass today, to attend the faith-formation class in the parish this evening, to pray together as husband and wife, to pursue a certain spiritual practice in the home, and the like — in time of spiritual desolation. His norm is clear and without exception: *never* make such changes. Two questions suffice: Am I in a time of spiritual desolation? And am I, in a time of spiritual desolation, thinking of changing a spiritual proposal that I had in place before this desolation began? Whenever the answer to these two questions is yes, then we know clearly that we should not make this change. On the contrary, Ignatius says, we should be "firm and constant" in what we had planned before the desolation began.

Ignatius then gives the reason for the norm: "Because, as in consolation the good spirit guides and counsels us more, so in desolation the bad spirit, with whose counsels we cannot find the way to a right decision." This is why we should never change our spiritual proposals when in spiritual desolation: because in spiritual desolation the enemy is speaking, counseling us to make such changes — the enemy "with whose counsels we *cannot* find the way to a right decision."

When I teach the rules, at this point I say, "If you were to forget everything else we say in this presentation, I beg of you never to forget rule 5. It will get you safely through almost any darkness you may encounter in life." Long and repeated experience, mine and that of many others, has shown the truth of this statement.

6

Alone in the Kitchen

Sixth Rule of Saint Ignatius

Although in desolation we should not change our first proposals, it is very advantageous to change ourselves intensely against the desolation itself, as by insisting more upon prayer, meditation, upon much examination, and upon extending ourselves in some suitable way of doing penance.

∞

Anne parked the car, entered the house, and stopped in the kitchen. She prepared coffee and sat at the table. It was 1:30 in the afternoon, and the house was empty. Mark was at work and the children at school.

Her morning as a special-education teacher had been trying. The problems of discipline with Steve, her special charge, had been worse than usual, and she had left school discouraged. Her best efforts seemed to make no difference, and she saw little progress in Steve.

Mark's continuing struggles also weighed on Anne. At times, she thought she saw improvement; at other times, things seemed the same or worse. Mark still refused to talk with her about it. The tension was affecting her sleep, contributing to the tiredness she felt.

Normally, at this time, Anne would pray with the Bible for some minutes. She especially loved the Psalms. The day before, she had begun praying with Psalm 27, "The LORD is my light and my salvation; whom should I fear?" (v. 1). The Bible, open to this psalm, lay at hand.

But now Anne felt little desire to pray. Other things drew her more: another check on Facebook; a look to see if e-mail had arrived; a glance at channels on television; a scroll through videos on YouTube; a phone conversation with Sally, always eager to talk, but whose conversation easily slipped into gossip; even food that she didn't need and that was not good for her.

Anne knew where all this would lead: it would solve nothing and would only leave her feeling emptier. In her sadness and discouragement, she lifted her heart to the Lord: "Jesus, be close to me now. You know that I am tired and discouraged and that I don't see clearly what to do. You know how alone I feel this afternoon. Be with me. Help me."

Anne's eye caught the open Bible. She reached for it and read the first verses of Psalm 27, "The LORD is my light and my salvation; whom should I fear? The Lord is my life's refuge; of whom should I be afraid? ... Though an army encamp against me, my heart does not fear. Though war be waged against me, even then do I trust" (vv. 1, 3). Again she prayed, "Jesus, be my light today. Be my salvation. Help me not to be afraid. Help me to trust." She remembered past times when she had made similar prayers and how the Lord had never abandoned her. Somehow she had always survived the hard times. As she remembered, Anne found it easier to believe that the Lord would not abandon her now.

Then Anne turned to the Lord and asked, "Jesus, what is happening this afternoon? What am I feeling? How did it get this way?" As she pondered, she perceived that the immediate cause of her discouragement was the difficult session with Steve. She simply did not know how to help him. Anne resolved that she would speak with her supervisor. This woman was experienced in such issues, and similar conversations in the past had been helpful. It was time for another. Having made this decision, Anne felt better.

Anne saw clearly that flight into mindless media, empty conversation, or unnecessary food would not help. She turned away from these and toward Psalm 27. Slowly she read the words, allowing their meaning to enter her heart. Some minutes later, she rose to attend to household tasks. When it was time, she left to bring the children home from school.

∞

This afternoon in the kitchen, Anne experiences spiritual desolation. To overcome it, she applies the spiritual tools Ignatius provides in rule 6:

> Although in desolation we should not change our first proposals, it is very advantageous to change ourselves intensely against the desolation itself, as by insisting more upon prayer, meditation, upon much examination, and upon extending ourselves in some suitable way of doing penance.

Though in time of spiritual desolation "we should not change our first proposals"—a summary of rule 5—we are not to remain passive. There are changes that we *should* make in spiritual desolation: not to our earlier proposals, but to *ourselves* and to how we are facing the desolation: "it is very advantageous to *change ourselves intensely* against the desolation itself." Ignatius supplies four means for these changes, classic means in the spiritual life but here applied specifically to the battle against spiritual desolation: "by insisting more upon *prayer, meditation,* upon *much examination,* and upon extending ourselves in some *suitable way of doing penance.*"

Discernment of Spirits in Marriage

Anne applies all four this afternoon in the kitchen:

- *Prayer*: in this context, by "prayer," Ignatius intends prayer of petition, that is, *simply to ask God's help*, and with God's help, that of our brothers and sisters in the communion of saints: Mary, the angels, our favorite saints, loved ones with the Lord. Anne does this at the kitchen table: "Jesus, be close to me now.... Be with me. Help me." Do we think to do this when, like Anne, we experience spiritual desolation? Jesus promises: "Ask and it will be given to you" (Matt. 7:7). These are not just words. This promise is real. In time of spiritual desolation, *ask for help*.

- *Meditation*: call to mind the truths of faith (God's love, his providence, Jesus's redeeming grace, and so many encouraging truths of our faith), verses of Scripture (Psalm 23; John 14:1; Phil. 4:13: the scriptural verses that most speak to your heart), and memories of God's faithful love in the past that can strengthen you now, in this struggle. Anne does this as well. She turns to a psalm she loves, Psalm 27, whose message encourages her to resist the desolation. She remembers past times of struggle and how God has never abandoned her. Can you meditate like this in times of spiritual desolation? If so, you will experience the strength such meditation brings.

- *Much examination*: two questions, both enormously helpful, to ask in times of desolation: "What am I feeling?" and "How did this begin?" When, like Anne, you struggle with desolation, prayerfully ask these two questions.

    "What am I feeling?" Simply to name the experience as spiritual desolation is greatly liberating. Now you know what is happening. Now you can plan how to deal with it.

"How did this begin?" If you can locate the origin of the spiritual desolation, the struggle reduces to manageable size. You cannot resist an overwhelming, crushing, all-encompassing cloud of desolation. You can resist a desolation that arose from a specific cause. When Anne perceives that her spiritual desolation stems from the difficult session with Steve, she can make decisions about this. She plans to meet with her supervisor, and her heart is lightened.

• *Suitable penance*: suitable, that is, apt to help resist the specific pull toward escape the person experiences in the desolation, a pull that can easily become "low and earthly." Thus, Anne does not turn to food when this would be unhealthy self-indulgence. She does not call Sally. She does not turn to the Internet, social media, or television. Such small gestures of penitential courage greatly assist the battle against spiritual desolation. When we perform them, we do exactly the opposite of what the spiritual desolation proposes — always a good thing!

What will happen if, in time of spiritual desolation at home, at work, commuting, preparing dinner, shopping, or in any aspect of your life, you turn to God with a prayer of petition for help; you call to mind truths of faith, biblical verses, and memories of God's fidelity in the past; you examine what you are feeling and how this began; and you stand your ground with small gestures of penitential courage? You may struggle with the desolation for a time, but the struggle will be easier and will end sooner. You will be on the road to freedom.

7

The Lie That Says, "You Can't"

Seventh Rule of Saint Ignatius

Let one who is in desolation consider how the Lord has left him in trial in his natural powers, so that he may resist the various agitations and temptations of the enemy; since he can resist with the divine help, which always remains with him, though he does not clearly feel it; for the Lord has taken away from him his great fervor, abundant love, and intense grace, leaving him, however, sufficient grace for eternal salvation.

∞

The children were in bed. Mark entered the kitchen, where Anne was finishing for the day.

"Could we talk?" he asked.

Anne understood immediately, and her heart lifted. "Yes," she said, "This is a good time."

They sat.

"I know it's been hard for you recently," Mark said, "and I want to apologize. I knew that you wanted to talk, but I felt that I just couldn't do it. You know that I've been slipping spiritually, and I've been ashamed of it. That's what made it hard to talk."

"I understand," Anne said. "I've had some struggles too."

"Have you? Spiritual struggles?"

"Oh, yes. I'll tell you about them. But right now I want to listen."

"It may sound strange," Mark said, "but it helps to know that you, too, struggle. I'll be glad to hear about it when you want to talk."

Anne nodded her appreciation but said nothing, letting Mark know that she was ready to listen.

"I think that the root of it all," Mark said, "is discouragement, that awful feeling that I can't do it, that I'll go back to what I was, that I won't be the husband you need and the father the children need. Jim really knows how to play on that. I see clearly that I need to end that relationship. I'm going to do it."

"I can't tell you how happy that makes me!" Anne replied. "I've longed for that. What's happened? What's changed?"

"I went to see Father Reed," Mark answered, "and he helped me understand a lot about all this. Speaking with him has made it easier to speak to you."

"Everything you say is good news. I'm so glad," Anne said.

For a moment both were silent. Both felt the tension of the past weeks lifting.

"Tell me," Anne continued, "What did Father Reed say?"

"He gave me words for what I've been experiencing. That helps me understand what's going on and makes a big difference in responding to it. Everything has seemed so confused, so dark. I couldn't make sense out of it, and I felt like I was too weak to overcome it. Father Reed calls it 'spiritual desolation' and says it's a normal tactic of the evil one — the 'enemy,' he calls him — in a person who is trying to grow spiritually. I have been trying, though not too well recently, to do that since the night Father spoke in the church."

"Yes, I know," Anne nodded, "and it's been wonderful to see. I think I know what you mean by spiritual desolation, because I've been experiencing it too."

"Have you? I didn't know."

"Yes, Mark. You're not alone in this."

"Well, if this is normal spiritual experience," Mark said wryly, "it's nice to know that I'm normal, and that I'm not the only one."

"If it's normal," Anne said with a smile, "then it's important."

"What do you mean?"

"If this is ordinary, daily experience in the spiritual life, then it matters. We need to know about it and how to deal with it."

"You're right," Mark said. "Well," he continued, "Father Reed homed in on the way I kept saying, 'I can't do it,' 'I'll never change,' 'I'm too weak,' 'Old habits die hard,' and other ways of saying the same thing. 'We need to remember,' Father said, 'that the struggle with spiritual desolation lies within God's providence in our lives, not outside of it. God allows this because, if we resist the desolation, we grow stronger in the spiritual life.'

"'But I'm not resisting it very well,' I said.

"'It's true,' he said, 'that it takes effort to resist spiritual desolation, and sometimes we have to struggle for a while. But the reason you feel defeated is that you've believed a lie. This lie says that you are defeated before you begin, that you are helpless, that "you can't do it," as you've been saying so often. Of course the enemy wants you to believe that!'"

"Father Reed quoted Saint Paul, 'God is faithful, and will not let you be tried beyond your strength' [1 Cor. 10:13]. Then he mentioned Saint Ignatius of Loyola and his counsel to remember, in time of desolation, when we're feeling that we can't, that in reality *we can*—we *can* pray, persevere, make spiritual progress, grow in God's service—because, even though we don't feel it in time of desolation, we know with the certitude of faith that God always gives us the grace we need to stay firmly on track. It's the same thing Saint Paul says."

"Yes," Anne said, "I see that."

"You know," Mark continued, "it really does make a difference. Father was right: I *was* feeling 'defeated before I began.' Just to know, on a deep level of faith, that God will always give me the grace I need to resist desolation makes me ready to begin the struggle again. This time I don't intend to lay it down. I'll need your help, and that's part of what I wanted to say tonight. I've been doing—or trying to do—this alone. I want that to change. I want you with me in this. Will you forgive the way I've been? And will you help me now?"

Mark looked and saw that Anne was moved. She reached out to him, and they embraced. "Yes," she said, "we will do it together."

∞

Without citing the text, Father Reed explains Ignatius's rule 7 to Mark:

> Let one who is in desolation consider how the Lord has left him in trial in his natural powers, so that he may resist the various agitations and temptations of the enemy; since he can resist with the divine help, which always remains with him, though he does not clearly feel it; for the Lord has taken away from him his great fervor, abundant love and intense grace, leaving him, however, sufficient grace for eternal salvation.

If we believe the "I can't" that the enemy insinuates in spiritual desolation, we are likely to give up, pull back, and surrender the journey of growth—precisely the enemy's purpose. This is the danger that, until he speaks with Father Reed and Anne, Mark faces. And so, Ignatius says, when you feel this "I can't," *consider* (ponder, recall, reflect on) three related truths that will greatly encourage you to continue:

• This time of spiritual desolation is a *trial*. Consider this difficult experience *on the level of faith*, where its truth is revealed. Your spiritual desolation this day, this evening, in this time of prayer, at home, at work, is a trial that the Lord, who loves you and whose providence guides your life, has permitted you to undergo (see Acts 14:22). Reflect that this burdensome time has meaning within God's loving design for you, that it is not useless pain.

• Further, consider the reason why God asks you to undergo this trial: so that you may resist the enemy's desolation. In fact, it is *by resisting* that we grow in the ability to resist. And if it is true, as I believe, that for most of us, spiritual desolation is a primary obstacle on the spiritual journey, then this ability is one of the greatest gifts God can give. Each time you undergo the trial of spiritual desolation and resist it, you grow stronger to resist it in the future.

• Finally, consider the fact that *you can resist* — that you are *not* destined helplessly to succumb, that you *can* come safely through this trial, because even though you do not feel it, you *know* with the firmness of faith that God is giving you all the grace you need to stand firm in this trial: "since he *can* resist with the divine help, which *always* remains with him."

Consider these three truths. Reflect on them. Ponder them. Take them deeply to heart, especially in time of spiritual desolation.

8

When Will the Darkness Pass?

Eighth Rule of Saint Ignatius

Let one who is in desolation work to be in patience, which is contrary to the vexations which come to him, and let him think that he will soon be consoled, diligently using the means against such desolation, as is said in the sixth rule.

∞

From Anne's journal, Tuesday, three months later:

> Mark and I continue to share about these spiritual ups
> and downs. He has met twice more with Father Reed,
> and he brings our questions there. We're both beginning
> to get a better feel for this daily spiritual experience. I see
> that, when we talk together about these things, even the
> dark times bring us closer.

From Mark's journal, Wednesday, one day later:

> What a strange thing to realize that the whole time I
> had the help I needed right here at home, and I was too
> ashamed, feeling too low, to turn to it. Anne has become
> my greatest strength as I continue to try and to struggle.
> It's not all perfect, and I slip at times, but never too far
> because Anne and I are talking regularly about this. I
> know she's happier, and I am too.

From Anne's journal, Monday afternoon, the following
week:

Discernment of Spirits in Marriage

I noticed a pattern today. I think it's important, and so I'll describe it here.

I've been tired the last few days. It's my allergies again, always at this time of year. Steve has been particularly difficult recently, and I've felt like I was at my wits' end. The chaos in the classroom has been hard to endure. Maybe it's this time of year, but the children have been cranky too.

I got up this morning and went downstairs. The others were still sleeping. I felt tired and foresaw a long and tiring day: the battle of getting the children up and ready for school; taking them there; then another demanding morning with Steve, the sulking, the shouting, the squirming, the refusal to learn; and then back home, more tired, to deal with everything again. It felt like this was going to be a long, long, difficult day.

Normally, when I'm up before the others, I pray. But this morning, I hardly wanted to. Mark's Father Reed would call it desolation, I suppose. I had to make myself do it. I asked the Lord to help me get through the day.

Now I'm home, waiting to pick up the children from school. The day has not gone as badly as I feared. I was able to cope with the tiredness, enough to do all that I needed to do. Steve was difficult, but not as difficult as I anticipated. He may actually have learned something today. When I turned to the Lord and asked his help, I felt him with me, and that gave me the patience, even the warmth, I needed. I feel ready for the children and Mark this evening.

The pattern seems to be this: You get into these dark times, these times of desolation, and you feel as though it's just going to continue, all day, all week, maybe even *forever if the darkness is heavy enough. Then you find that it doesn't. It ends sooner, usually a lot sooner than the darkness wants you to believe. If you do believe that it's going to go on and on, you get pretty discouraged, and you may give up in small or greater ways. But if you realize that it's not going to last, certainly not as long as it wants you to believe, it's a lot easier to get through it. I'll share this with Mark this evening.*

From Mark's journal, that same evening:

When we spoke, Anne made a good point. If I can remember it when I feel desolate, it will help me. When I think back, the sense that the darkness will just go on and on is a big part of what made it so hard to resist. You start looking for compensations. At least, I did. I'll raise this with Father Reed next time we meet. I bet he'll smile and say that Anne is catching on quickly.

Ignatius writes in rule 8:

> Let one who is in desolation work to be in patience, which is contrary to the vexations that come to him, and let him think that he will soon be consoled, diligently using the means against such desolation, as is said in the sixth rule.

"Let him think that he will *soon* be consoled." The adverb "soon" in this rule is powerful. Ignatius says that when you are in spiritual desolation, the desolation—that is, the enemy—wants you to believe that this will continue for a long and perhaps a very long time. If you believe this, the desolation will be hard to resist. And so, in time of spiritual desolation, *think about* (consider, call to mind) this truth: my present desolation will not last as long as the enemy wants me to believe. In fact, it will end *soon*. To know that the desolation you are experiencing today, this morning, this evening, will end, and end much sooner than the enemy wishes you to believe, fortifies you greatly to resist it. Anne perceives this truth when she reviews her experience on the Monday described.

Such awareness helps us to be *patient*, to not give in, to not surrender to the desolation, but to finish the time of prayer, to pursue the task at hand, to carry on faithfully with the work, the service, and the commitments of the day. The desolation, Ignatius adds, will pass the more quickly if you apply the four tools provided in rule 6: prayer of petition, meditation, much examination, and suitable gestures of penitential courage.

9

Why Does God Permit Spiritual Desolation?

Ninth Rule of Saint Ignatius

There are three principal causes for which we find ourselves desolate. The first is because we are tepid, slothful, or negligent in our spiritual exercises, and so through our faults spiritual consolation withdraws from us. The second, to try us and see how much we are and how much we extend ourselves in his service and praise without so much payment of consolations and increased graces. The third, to give us true recognition and understanding so that we may interiorly feel that it is not ours to attain or maintain increased devotion, intense love, tears, or any other spiritual consolation, but that all is the gift and grace of God our Lord, and so that we may not build a nest in something belonging to another, raising our mind in some pride or vainglory, attributing to ourselves the devotion or the other parts of the spiritual consolation.

∞

It was Sunday afternoon, two months later. Lunch was finished, and the children were scattered, busy with their various occupations. Mark and Anne sat in the living room, talking.

Matters of family and work arose in the conversation. Then, as occurred more often these days, Mark raised a question regarding a spiritual experience.

"You know," he said, "that I continue to struggle with desolation from time to time."

"Yes," Anne said, "and so do I. I thought Father Reed said this was normal in the spiritual life."

"It's hard to doubt it," Mark answered, "because we all seem to experience it at times. But that's not my question now. It concerns something else about desolation.

"I was pretty far from God for several years. That was my choice, and it was wrong. That darkness was my own fault. God gave me the grace to see it and try to change, and I'm grateful. I've been trying for some time, probably more than ever this past year."

Anne nodded.

"But the times of desolation still happen. Why? They can be hard, and there's always the danger of giving in — I have sometimes. I'm trying the best I can to change my life. Basically, I'm living with God; at least I think so. So why do these times of desolation still happen?

"It's a good question," Anne replied, "and I'm not sure I know the answer. It seems to me that another question underlies it: Why does a God who loves us, and whom we are trying to love, allow times of desolation that he could spare us? God is all-loving and all-powerful. Desolation, Father Reed says, is a tactic of the enemy to try to dishearten us. If God loves us, then why does he allow the enemy to burden us with desolation?"

"You put it more clearly than I did. Yes, that's the question, and the answer matters to me. It's confusing to try your best and find that you can still feel desolate in the spiritual life. I'll ask Father Reed the next time we talk."

∽

From Mark's journal, ten days later:

> I met today with Father Reed. He moved slowly and seemed a little weaker. I raised the question that Anne and I had discussed. He smiled and commented that we were asking good questions.
>
> He answered that there are several reasons why a God who loves us — and precisely because he loves us — permits the enemy to bring these times of desolation. While it's true that I am trying to grow spiritually and that growth is happening, there are times when I regress in one area or another: prayer slips, I open myself to things that are not good for me, I start to get self-centered with Anne or the children, or other areas of regression. God loves me too much, Father says, simply to allow this to happen. At such times,

*experiences of spiritual desolation serve as a wake-up call.
They can lead me to see and correct what has weakened.
He's right about this, and I see it in my experience.*

*But, he continued, there are other reasons why God,
again very much because he loves us, permits the enemy
to bring spiritual desolation, and these have nothing to do
with faults on my part. Father pointed out that while much
growth comes through the energy of spiritual consolation,
other kinds of growth normally come through the struggle
with desolation. Looking back over these past years, I see
this too. Sometimes the darkest times have led me to take the
most fruitful spiritual steps.*

*Then, Father says, the struggle with desolation keeps us
humble and helps us avoid complacency and self-satisfaction
in the spiritual life. True humility, he says, is a good spiritual
space in which to be—like Mary, who speaks with joy of
her low estate, or Jesus, who is humble of heart.*

*It's a good answer, though I still find times of desolation
hard. Resisting desolation is easier when I know that these
times have meaning, that God permits them for reasons of
growth, and that growth will come if, with the help of his
grace, I do resist them.*

*Father suggested that I consider looking at Saint Ignatius
of Loyola's rules for discernment. He said that the questions
that Anne and I have been raising are dealt with there. I
should look at these rules.*

∞

Mark and Anne raise a good question: Why does a God who loves
us permit the enemy to bring these discouraging experiences of
spiritual desolation? He could spare us such times: Why doesn't

he? Have you ever asked this question? Have you ever wondered about this when you struggle to pray or live the spiritual life?

Ignatius recognizes the importance of this question and addresses it in rule 9. He writes:

> There are three principal causes for which we find ourselves desolate.

"Cause" here indicates God's reason for permitting the spiritual desolation.

A first reason:

> The first is because we are tepid, slothful or negligent in our spiritual exercises, and so through our faults spiritual consolation withdraws from us.

A person may be generally progressing toward God but may, as Father Reed indicates, begin to regress in one or another area. Then God, "who loves me more than I love myself" (Ignatius), may permit us to experience spiritual desolation. The discomfort of the desolation alerts us to the area of regression and so helps us reintegrate it into our growth toward God.

A second reason:

> The second, to try us and see how much we are and how much we extend ourselves in his service and praise without so much payment of consolations and increased graces.

At times, even when we are not at fault, God may permit spiritual desolation because we grow spiritually in key ways when we struggle against it. Through that struggle, we are strengthened and we progress in the spiritual life.

A third reason:

> The third, to give us true recognition and understanding so that we may interiorly feel that it is not ours to attain or maintain increased devotion, intense love, tears, or any other spiritual consolation, but that all is the gift and grace of God our Lord, and so that we may not build a nest in something belonging to another, raising our mind in some pride or vainglory, attributing to ourselves the devotion or the other parts of the spiritual consolation.

The experience of spiritual desolation teaches us that all spiritual consolation is God's gift—we know this surely when burdened by spiritual desolation!—and so keeps us humble, with the many spiritual blessings that follow (see Matt. 5:3).

Mark says, "Resisting desolation is easier when I know that these times have meaning, that God permits them for reasons of growth." This is Ignatius's point in rule 9.

In fact, when God permits spiritual desolation, he *uses the enemy against himself*. Through the struggle against desolation, we are healed (from areas of regression), we grow (through the trial), and we avoid a pitfall (complacency). In all this, God's love is richly at work.

10

Before the Struggle Begins

Tenth Rule of Saint Ignatius

Let the one who is in consolation think how he will conduct himself in the desolation which will come after, taking new strength for that time.

∞

Mark walked down the aisle, found his seat, and prepared for the flight. Ten minutes later, the plane taxied to the runway. He was returning from the annual conference of the American Optometric Association. Before boarding, he and Anne had spoken by phone, and his heart was still warmed by their conversation. It showed him once again that they were growing closer. They had spoken daily during this trip, and her joy in these conversations told him that she missed him and looked forward to his return. During the call, his daughter Maria and son Patrick had also spoken briefly, both, in their different ways, expressing the same.

The plane took off, and Mark settled into the routine of flying. But he was not ready to resume work or watch the in-flight entertainment. He sat for several minutes, simply grateful for what his life was becoming. As he sat, he felt the Lord close to him. Above all, he felt the Lord's love.

A prayer rose from his heart: "Lord, thank you for the goodness of what is happening in my life. It is so much more than I dreamed possible even a few years ago. I bless you for Anne and the children. I bless you that you've guided me safely through the times of struggle and desolation. You never abandoned me when I was in darkness. I know that you will be with me in future struggles and that you will see me through. Lord, strengthen me for those times. Help me not to give in to them. Be close to me. Show me how to respond to them, and give me the grace to do it." Peace and a sense of safety filled his heart.

A thought came. Mark remembered Anne's comments about Psalm 27. He took his phone, opened the Kindle app, and found the Bible. He read the first words of the psalm, the words that Anne had cited, "The LORD is my light and my salvation; whom should I fear? The LORD is my life's refuge; of whom should I be afraid?" These words spoke to him, and he understood more deeply what they meant for Anne: How could he fear when the Lord loved him, was close to him, was his light, his help, and his stronghold?

Mark decided that in future times of discouragement he would say these words. He highlighted them in the text and repeated them slowly three times, to fix them in his memory. After his trip, he would tell Anne about this. He knew she would be happy to hear it. He would also suggest that, in times of desolation, each tell the other and that they pray these words together.

∞

From Mark's journal the next evening:

I spoke with Anne, and we will use Psalm 27 for mutual support in times of struggle. The more we share about these things, the stronger we both become. It makes such a difference not to be alone in time of desolation.

I thought again about that prayer on the plane. I realize that it is helpful, in times when my heart is at peace and God feels close, to think about future struggles with discouragement and to prepare for them. I think that praying like

this, asking God for help in future desolation, and praying
with the verses from the psalm, will make a difference. I can
do this while commuting, while exercising, when I pray, and
in free moments here and there. Anne and I could also do
this together. I think this would really help.

∞

Mark is right. In his tenth rule. Ignatius writes:

> Let the one who is in consolation think how he will
> conduct himself in the desolation which will come
> after, taking new strength for that time.

Like Mark and Anne, we all experience times of spiritual consolation and times of spiritual desolation. As we have said, this
is normal in the spiritual life. What matters, Ignatius repeats, is
to be aware of these changing states, to recognize the one as of
God and the other as of the enemy, and to accept the one and
reject the other.

In rule 10, Ignatius highlights a further fruit to be gained
from times of spiritual consolation. The primary call in such
times—an uplifting, warm time of prayer; a day of grace and
blessing; a week of peace in the Lord—is simply to *receive* the
joy, strength, hope, and energy that God infuses through this
gift. Never let anything weigh on your freedom to receive, to
be loved! But if, like Mark, in times of spiritual consolation we
also look ahead and prepare for future spiritual desolation, that
desolation will be easier to reject when it comes. If, according
to their plan, Mark and Anne do this together, their preparation
will be all the stronger.

Discernment of Spirits in Marriage

Have you ever done this? Mark's proposal is a good one. Individually, on the plane, and later together with Anne when they speak, Mark "takes new strength" for future desolation. Try this. You will love the results.

11

Finding Our Balance

Eleventh Rule of Saint Ignatius

Let one who is consoled seek to humble himself and lower himself as much as he can, thinking of how little he is capable in the time of desolation without such grace or consolation. On the contrary, let one who is in desolation think that he can do much with God's sufficient grace to resist all his enemies, taking strength in his Creator and Lord.

∾

Three months later, Saturday morning:

The sun shone on the walkers, joggers, and bikers. It was midmorning, and Mark and Anne were walking in the park. Anne's mother was with the children.

The past weeks had been too busy for a real chance to talk, and they welcomed their unhurried time together this morning. As they walked, they spoke of various matters. Then Anne said, "Mark, you've seemed a little more tired recently."

"Yes," Mark replied, "I'd say that's true. You don't miss much!"

"Are things busier at work?"

"No. They are always about as busy as they can be."

"Then what's happening? Aren't you feeling well?"

"I think I'm fine."

"I've noticed," Anne said, "that you are rising earlier in the mornings."

"Yes," Mark answered, "prayer has felt blessed in these past months, and I find that I want more than ten minutes with the Scriptures."

"How long are you spending now?"

"You know, I haven't timed it. Maybe twenty minutes, probably more sometimes. I rise earlier so that I won't have to interrupt prayer when it seems so fruitful."

"I see," Anne said.

Later in the walk, Anne asked about the prayer breakfast. "A few weeks ago, you mentioned that Father asked you to join the team that chooses the speakers and prepares the breakfast. How is that going?"

"Quite well," Mark said, "and I like being part of the team. I'm getting to know the others better, and the whole experience seems richer."

"What do they want you to do?"

"They asked me to find the speakers. It takes a bit of research and some phoning, but the men have been pleased with the results. It's a learning experience for me, too, and my conversations with the speakers are interesting."

They completed the circuit of the park and began a second. Both were enjoying their time together.

Anne told Mark that a change in her teaching schedule would make it easier to get to Mass during the week. "You said that you wanted to try going to Mass on your lunch hour," Anne said. "Is that working out?"

"Yes. It means a full lunch hour because of the drive over and back, and sometimes the Mass goes a little longer. Also because sometimes things take longer than expected with a patient. But, yes, I like it. It's such a blessing to have Mass more often during the week, and I feel the difference."

"What about lunch?"

"That has to be quick," Mark admitted.

Anne stopped and faced Mark. "Are you doing any other spiritual things these days?"

"Well, yes," Mark said. "One of the speakers recommended Saint Francis de Sales's *Introduction to the Devout Life*, and I've been listening to it on audio book during the commute. It's the best thing I've read on the spiritual life in the lay and married vocation. It's given me some ideas of things we could do to grow spiritually, you and I, and the family, and I want to share them with you."

They had reached a park bench. "Mark, let's stop for a few minutes," Anne said. They sat and looked out over the lake before them.

"Mark," Anne said, "you know how happy I am about what is happening spiritually for you, and I love what it's doing for our marriage and our family. I know that you've felt spiritually alive these past few months, and everything you've told me is good. But I wonder how long you can keep all of this up. You get less sleep. Your lunch is rushed. You are busier. You've gotten more tired. Choosing the speakers takes time, and we both know how packed things are at work. Now you're thinking of adding more. All of it's good, but what about you? What's going to happen if you get too worn?"

Mark was silent for a moment. "That's a good question," he said at last. "You know, I never saw the whole picture the way you just put it together. I've had a wonderful sense of God's love and closeness in these weeks, and each new thing seemed to come naturally. I enjoy them all and look forward to them. But I can't argue with you: you're right. Things are getting too pressured."

"I wonder," Anne said, "if this isn't another aspect of the spiritual experience we've been talking about. We've said a lot about not giving in to desolation and the sense of helplessness it wants to instill. But maybe there's also something to be said about times of consolation, that we not stretch too far in times of energy and wind up getting hurt spiritually in another way."

Discernment of Spirits in Marriage

"I think you're on to something, Anne," Mark replied. He smiled. "If you keep this up, pretty soon you'll be giving Father Reed a run for his money."

∞

Anne has traced what I would call the "portrait of the mature person of discernment." This person neither undertakes too much in time of spiritual consolation nor succumbs to hopelessness in time of spiritual desolation. Humble in consolation and trusting in desolation, this person forges ahead in the spiritual life amid the alternations of both.

In rule 11, Ignatius writes:

> Let one who is consoled seek to humble himself and lower himself as much as he can, thinking of how little he is capable in the time of desolation without such grace or consolation. On the contrary, let one who is in desolation think that he can do much with God's sufficient grace to resist all his enemies, taking strength in his Creator and Lord.

All that Ignatius has said in the rules is intended to help us grow toward this portrait.

Do you ever push too hard in time of spiritual consolation in your efforts to grow, in new undertakings, in further demands on your energies? Do you ever lose heart when spiritual desolation weighs and you hear its discouraging lies? In both cases, rule 11 points the way: maintain wise limits in time of consolation, and trust without faltering in time of desolation.

12

The Easiest Way to Resist Temptation

Twelfth Rule of Saint Ignatius

The enemy acts as spoiled children do in being weak when faced with strength and strong when faced with weakness. For it is proper to spoiled children, when they begin to act out, to lose heart and desist when their parents confront them firmly; and, on the contrary, if their parents respond with weakness and help-lessness, their acting out grows greatly and knows no bounds.[2] In the same way, it is proper to the enemy to weaken and lose heart, fleeing and ceasing his temptations when the person who is exercising himself in spiritual things confronts the temptations of the enemy firmly, doing what is diametrically opposed to them; and, on the contrary, if the person who is exercising himself begins to be afraid and lose heart in suffering the temptations, there is no beast so fierce on the face of the earth as the enemy of human nature in following out his damnable intention with such growing malice.

[2] I have changed Ignatius's metaphor here to avoid distraction from the point he wishes to illustrate. David Fleming, SJ, adopts the metaphor of the spoiled child in *Draw Me into Your Friendship* (Saint Louis: Institute of Jesuit Sources, 1996), 257.

∞

From Anne's journal, Wednesday, six months later:

Mark's company has been bought out by a larger one.
They are all worried about their jobs. Mark, too, is
waiting to see what will happen. It may mean no change,
they might ask him to relocate, or he could simply lose his
job, though that doesn't seem likely.

From Anne's journal, Tuesday, three weeks later:

Today at school they told me that, for budgetary reasons,
they may have to reduce my hours. I told Mark, and he
listened well, but both of us are aware of the financial
issues involved, all the more if his job situation changes.
It could affect our healthcare coverage, the children's
schooling, and other plans we've made.

From Anne's journal, Thursday, two weeks later:

Still no clarity about our jobs. We keep waiting to find
out. I'm trying to pray more, but sometimes it's hard to

stop worrying. With these anxieties always in the back-
ground, it gets harder to deal with daily issues at home,
with the children, even with Mark.

From Anne's journal, Wednesday, one week later:

I called Sally today, and we spoke for a half hour. I know
that it's not good for me, but she's always a listening ear
and ready to talk. It's usually that early afternoon hour
when I'm alone in the house. Today I was feeling too
alone, and all the concerns were there.

From Anne's journal, Tuesday, one week later:

I've spoken with Mark about these worries, and he
listens. He tries not to show it, but I know that he's wor-
ried too. I don't know if our conversations are helping in
the way I need. I don't want to show too much anxiety
either, because he needs my support.

From Anne's journal, Friday, three days later:

Sally and I have talked three times this week. Each time,
the calls get a little longer. I don't know how she has the
time for this. I know I don't. I wind up taking too long
to get things done for the children and around the house.
But it's a relief to talk to someone when you feel alone.

From Anne's journal, Monday, three days later:

The calls with Sally are getting more frequent and last-
ing longer. It was an hour today. These conversations

distract me from the worries, and that's why I turn to
them, but they leave me empty. The longer the conversation goes on, the harder I find it to stop. And it always
spirals downward in one way or another. It leaves me
thinking about things that are not good for me and judg-
ing other people. I also find that I have less desire to pray
after we speak and less patience with the children.

*This early-afternoon time used to be my time for
prayer, but that's getting less frequent and especially in a
time when I need prayer more.*

From Anne's journal, Wednesday, two days later:

*Still no word on our jobs. This evening I told Mark about
what I'm feeling and the phone calls with Sally. I didn't
try to hide my worry about our financial situation. I told
him that the calls with Sally are increasing and that they
diminish my energy to deal with things. They also mean
that I'm praying less.*

*This conversation was different from those we've had re-
cently. I think Mark appreciated my openness, and it helped
him be open too. He told me about something he's learned in
his struggle to avoid using the phone in the wrong way — another phone issue! He meant the temptation, in time of
discouragement, to view harmful things on the phone. It's a
question he's talked about with Father Reed.*

*Mark said that, in this different matter, he noticed
something similar to what I'd said about my conversations
with Sally. The beginning is usually fairly innocuous:
news sites, even Catholic ones, then sports, then . . . this
was where things could get worse. He found that once he*

was into it, he didn't want to stop. Mildly objectionable things would lead to worse things, like a snowball rolling down a mountainside, getting harder and harder to stop, and more and more likely to run him over. Father Reed helped him see that the surest and easiest way to avoid this was never to start, because it's true that the longer it goes on, the harder it gets to stop. Mark said that he's been trying to do this, just not reach out for the phone at those times, and that it does make it a lot easier.

That fits with my experience with Sally, and I said this to Mark. It means, I think, that I have to stop calling Sally, and that if she calls, I need to end the conversation as soon as I can without being rude. I think she'll get the message pretty quickly.

∞

This is exactly the point of Ignatius's twelfth rule. He offers a metaphor and then draws from it the lesson he wants us to see. The metaphor:

> The enemy acts as spoiled children do in being weak when faced with strength and strong when faced with weakness. For it is proper to spoiled children, when they begin to act out, to lose heart and desist when their parents confront them firmly; and, on the contrary, if their parents respond with weakness and helplessness, their acting out grows greatly and knows no bounds.

The enemy is "*weak* when faced with *strength* and *strong* when faced with *weakness*." This is what Ignatius wants to highlight.

Now the application of the metaphor to the enemy's temptations:

> In the same way, it is proper to the enemy to weaken and lose heart, fleeing and ceasing his temptations when the person who is exercising himself in spiritual things confronts the temptations of the enemy firmly, doing what is diametrically opposed to them; and, on the contrary, if the person who is exercising himself begins to be afraid and lose heart in suffering the temptations, there is no beast so fierce on the face of the earth as the enemy of human nature in following out his damnable intention with such growing malice.

If we are strong in resisting the enemy's temptations, if we stand firm *right in the very beginning* ("Why don't you let your prayer go till later?" "*No*, I always pray at this time, and I am going to pray exactly as I planned."), the enemy's weakness is revealed. But if we are weak in resisting when the temptation first begins ("Why don't you let your prayer go till later?" "*Yes*, maybe I could.... I don't really feel like it now.... Maybe later would be better ..."), the temptation will grow in strength and become increasingly hard to resist—the snowball effect Mark mentions. In this event, we are likely to succumb. Will, for example, the person who does not stop this temptation in its beginning but who dallies with it, ever pray that day?

Ask for the grace, and make the effort to resist temptations of any kind *in their very beginning*. Your life will grow easier, and you will be spared much suffering. Ignatius's rule 12 is a jewel that can bless your entire spiritual life.

13

To Speak Is to Defeat the Enemy

Thirteenth Rule of Saint Ignatius

Likewise he conducts himself as a false lover in wishing to remain secret and not be revealed. For a dissolute man who, speaking with evil intention, makes dishonorable advances to a daughter of a good father or a wife of a good husband, wishes his words and persuasions to be secret, and the contrary displeases him very much, when the daughter reveals to her father or the wife to her husband his false words and depraved intention, because he easily perceives that he will not be able to succeed with the undertaking begun. In the same way, when the enemy of human nature brings his wiles and persuasions to the just soul, he wishes and desires that they be received and kept in secret; but when one reveals them to one's good confessor or to another spiritual person, who knows his deceits and malicious designs, it weighs on him very much, because he perceives that he will not be able to succeed with the malicious undertaking he has begun, since his manifest deceits have been revealed.

∞

Eight months later, an e-mail from Mark's dad to Mark:

*Hi, Mark. I hope things are well. If you, Anne, and the
kids don't have any plans yet, Mom and I want to invite
you to join us for Thanksgiving. It's been a while, and it
would be nice to get together. Let me know what you think.
Dad."*

∞

Two days later:

"I had an e-mail from Dad," Mark said.

Anne understood that something was troubling Mark. "What
did he say?"

"He is inviting us to bring the family over for Thanksgiving."

"What do you think?"

"Anne," Mark said, "do you have time now to talk?"

"Yes, this is a good time." They sat together.

"You know that my relationship with my dad has never been
good. I've never found it easy to talk about. I've just wanted to
avoid it."

"I know," Anne replied, "and I've tried to respect that."

"I know, and I'm grateful. But something has changed, and now I need to talk about this."

Anne nodded.

"I don't want to exaggerate things," Mark began. "Dad was faithful, and he raised us according to what he thought was good for us. But he could be harsh. I never knew when I'd see that side of him, and I learned early on to keep my distance. I'll just share one incident, but it can stand for many similar experiences."

Mark was silent, remembering. "In the summers, we often went to the city pool to swim. This day it was crowded, and we were there, having a good time. Then Dad came. He told me to climb up the high diving board. I didn't want to. I was afraid. In front of all the others, he made me do it. Then he told me to dive. I was too scared. He began yelling. Everyone stopped and watched. It was a horrible moment. He just kept it up until finally I dove. When I got out of the water he berated me for my fear—you know, men have to be courageous, all of that—and then told me that he was doing this for my own good.

"I could tell you of other times like that, but you can see why I was uneasy around Dad. I never knew what was coming next, and I always felt that I couldn't live up to his expectations."

Mark stopped. He could see that Anne was absorbing his words. He looked at her and said quietly, "Thank you."

"So," he continued, "I've never made an issue of it, and I've never spoken to Dad about it. I've just kept my distance. I never take any initiative to spend time with him. It's been like that for years."

"And now?" Anne asked.

"Now I'm praying with the Bible, and some things I find there are hitting home. One passage came up for prayer the same day I got Dad's e-mail."

Mark reached for the Bible and opened it. "It's here," he said, "where Saint Paul speaks of 'bearing with one another and forgiving one another, if one has a grievance against another; as the Lord has forgiven you, so must you also do' (Col. 3:13). Last Sunday, too, the Gospel was about loving your enemies, and Father preached about that. I couldn't help thinking of my dad. Later in the Mass, when we prayed the Our Father and said the words, 'Forgive us our trespasses as we forgive those who trespass against us,' my dad came to mind again. He does now every time I say the Our Father.

"But I'm feeling torn. The need for distance from my dad is deep, and I can't just dismiss it. At the same time, I think the Lord is asking something more from me in regard to my dad. This keeps coming up when I pray, and I can't dismiss this either. Thoughts are also starting to come: 'You aren't much of a follower of Jesus. You don't live the way you talk. Maybe you'll never be a real follower of Jesus' — you know what these thoughts are like."

"Yes," Anne said. "So what do you think you need to do?"

"Well, right now I'm doing the first thing I need to do — that is, talking to you. And here's another thing. It seems obvious that if I talked to Father Reed about this, it would help. I've wanted to. I've seen him twice in the last two months, and both times I had planned to talk about my relationship with Dad."

"Did you?"

"No."

"Why not?"

Mark looked at Anne and smiled a little wryly. "You always ask the right question."

"I didn't," he continued, "because I was afraid to. That's as honest as I can be. I didn't because this is so deep, and it's not pretty. And now that you ask, maybe because I thought Father Reed would think less of me, that he'd be kind, but he'd lose respect for me. And perhaps also because he, too, is a kind of father, and I still find it hard to share sensitive things with a father. I've never had any experience in doing that."

"Mark," Anne said, "that is such an honest answer. I think you're already on the way to something new with your dad."

"Are you so sure," she continued, "that you can't be open with Father Reed? Yes, he's a spiritual father, but you've been sharing difficult things with him for a long time. Has he ever been harsh or belittling?"

"No, of course not."

"Then why don't you talk to him about your dad and what you've been feeling recently? Here's what I think. I think that as long as you keep this bottled up inside and don't speak about it—I mean to the right persons—you'll continue to struggle. But when you do talk about it, you'll begin to find freedom. That's why I'm so happy that you're sharing this right now. And that's why I think you need to call Father Reed, set a time to talk with him, and when you do, speak as openly as you have this evening."

Mark nodded his agreement. "It will not be easy," he said, "but I'll do it."

"I don't think you'll find it as hard as you fear," Anne replied. "You're already more than halfway there."

∞

From Mark's journal, a week later:

I spoke with Father Reed today. This time I did talk about my dad. I feel like a heavy burden has been lifted. Prayer is easier

*now. The tension and the inner accusations are gone. I'm glad
I spoke with Anne and Father Reed. I think this is also a lesson learned for the future when I feel burdens like this: speaking about them with the right person makes a big difference.*

*Will it be any easier this time with Dad than in the past?
I don't know. All I do know is that I'll try to be more open
to him. I'll do my best.*

E-mail from Mark to his father, the next day:

*Hi, Dad. Thanks for your message and for the invitation to
come for Thanksgiving. We'll be glad to. Just let us know
when you'd like us to be there. Again, thanks, and we'll see
you soon, Mark."*

∞

Earlier I said that, if you were to forget everything else in this
book, I begged of you never to forget rule 5. I affirmed that it
would guide you safely through almost any darkness you might
encounter on the spiritual journey. Now I will complete that
statement. I beg of you never to forget rules 5 and 13 together.
These two rules—do not make changes in the darkness of desolation, and speak to a wise and competent spiritual person about
the burdens in your heart—will bring you safely through any
darkness you may ever experience in your spiritual life.

What if Mark had not spoken openly with Anne? What if he
had not spoken openly with Father Reed? How long might the
burden have persisted? How much might it have weakened his
spiritual energy and hindered his spiritual growth?

In rule 13, Ignatius again provides a metaphor from which
he draws a spiritual lesson. He writes:

> Likewise he [the enemy] conducts himself as a false lover in wishing to remain secret and not be revealed. For a dissolute man who, speaking with evil intention, makes dishonorable advances to a daughter of a good father or a wife of a good husband, wishes his words and persuasions to be secret, and the contrary displeases him very much, when the daughter reveals to her father or the wife to her husband his false words and depraved intention, because he easily perceives that he will not be able to succeed with the undertaking begun.

In this rule, Ignatius highlights a further quality of the enemy in his temptations: when he brings these temptations, he wishes that *they remain secret and not be revealed*. As long as the woman says nothing, the selfish purpose of the false lover can proceed. But *in the moment itself* that she speaks to her father or husband about his "dishonorable advances," the false lover's efforts will be undone. His game will be up, and he will be helpless to proceed further.

Now the application of the metaphor:

> In the same way, when the enemy of human nature brings his wiles and persuasions to the just soul, he wishes and desires that they be received and kept in secret; but when one reveals them to one's good confessor or to another spiritual person, who knows his deceits and malicious designs, it weighs on him very much, because he perceives that he will not be able to succeed with the malicious undertaking he has begun, since his manifest deceits have been revealed.

The key is the contrast between the enemy's tactic and the response that Ignatius proposes: on the one hand, secrecy; on the other, open sharing with a wise and competent spiritual person. When the enemy brings his "wiles and persuasions," that is, his troubling burdens and temptations, "to the just soul," in this case to Mark, "he wishes and desires that they be received and kept *in secret*": that Mark, for example, say nothing about how his relationship with his father burdens his spiritual life. As long as Mark does not speak, the enemy's "game" can go on, and the likelihood of harm will increase.

"But," Ignatius continues, "when one reveals them [the enemy's burdens and temptations] to one's good confessor or to another spiritual person who knows his deceits and malicious designs" this "weighs on him very much" because "he knows that he will not be able to succeed with the malicious undertaking he has begun." Thus, when Mark speaks openly with Anne and Father Reed, the enemy's troubling temptations are vanquished. He is defeated, and Mark is set free.

Mark and all like him who experience the enemy's burdens do need to speak — but not just to anyone. Ignatius outlines two profiles of the person with whom one might speak: "one's good confessor" or "another spiritual person." What makes this confessor "good" and this person "spiritual" is that this confessor and this person "know his deceits and malicious designs" — that is, know, are familiar with, are conversant with, the enemy's maneuvers and tactics, and so are competent to assist those who approach them seeking help.

∞

Where can we find the right person or persons with whom to speak? I offer some concrete suggestions:

Discernment of Spirits in Marriage

- If ongoing spiritual direction with a wise and competent spiritual person is possible, avail yourself of this opportunity when you can. Mark meets with Father Reed, and this makes all the difference.

- The sacrament of Reconciliation is available to us all. Find a wise, competent confessor, go regularly to Confession and, when possible, to this same priest. The relationship of spiritual accompaniment that results is enormously beneficial.

- Make an annual retreat: a weekend, a day, part of a day—whatever is possible in your circumstances. In addition to their other benefits, retreats frequently offer a time to speak with a wise and competent spiritual person.

- Talk with a spiritual friend or group of friends. This is not formal spiritual direction, but such conversations can be very strengthening. A weekly phone call, a video conversation, or a meal together, with this focus, can help greatly.

- Join a spiritual group. Many are available in parishes and other institutions in the Church. This form of accompaniment is also strengthening, as, for example, the prayer breakfast is for Mark. Is there a group of faith formation, Bible study, or spiritual formation available to you?

- In marriage, another form of accompaniment, available only in this vocation, is offered: husbands and wives, without attempting to be each other's spiritual directors, can encourage each other, as Anne and Mark learn to do. Such mutual encouragement is an enormous blessing for a marriage and a family.

14

The Most Vulnerable Place—and How to Strengthen It

Fourteenth Rule of Saint Ignatius

Likewise he conducts himself as a leader, intent upon conquering and robbing what he desires. For, just as a captain and leader of an army in the field, pitching his camp and exploring the fortifications and defenses of a stronghold, attacks it at the weakest point, in the same way the enemy of human nature, roving about, looks in turn at all our theological, cardinal and moral virtues; and where he finds us weakest and most in need for our eternal salvation, there he attacks us and attempts to take us.

∞

All year, Anne had striven to help Steve progress. His special needs were significant, and she had never worked with a more difficult student. In recent months, encouraging signs had appeared. Steve was less disruptive and less prone to outbursts. Anne felt that, on some level, he sensed her sincere care for him and was responding. He was learning and was pleased to realize it.

Anne's supervisor was also aware of the change in Steve. One day she met Anne in the hall, stopped her, and told her how much she appreciated her work. A month later, she asked if Anne would be willing to teach Kathy, a problematic student with whom no one was willing to work. Anne agreed. As the weeks passed, Kathy, too, improved. For the first time, this young girl whose life had been so difficult, was learning to trust. As she did, her natural talents began to blossom.

Anne's colleagues marveled at her skill with these troubled children. Occasionally, some asked her advice. As the semester unfolded, more of them did so.

One day, the principal asked to speak with Anne. She told Anne that she was concerned about several new teachers who were struggling. They were so discouraged that they were close to quitting. The school, the principal said, could not afford to lose teachers at this point in the year. She proposed that Anne offer these teachers a weekly hour of mentoring, providing them a forum in which to discuss their problems and find guidance. The hour would continue as long as needed throughout the semester. Anne's salary would be correspondingly raised. The principal asked Anne to consider this possibility. Anne agreed to do so.

That evening, Anne spoke with Mark. He asked her how she felt about it. Anne said that she was honored to have been asked. She believed that the mentoring could be fruitful, and the increased salary would be welcome, especially with the earlier talk of shortened hours. She thought that she could add an hour a week without excessive strain. They agreed that Anne would accept, and she communicated her willingness to the principal.

A week passed, then two. Anne heard no more about the proposal. She grew frustrated and then angry. If they would not pursue their end of the project, she was not going to reach out to them. They had asked her to take on further work in an already busy life. If they were so casual about their own proposal, then so be it. There would be no mentoring. She, certainly, was not going to approach them.

Another week of silence passed. Anne found herself still more frustrated. At times, her irritation grew strong, and her mind churned with angry thoughts. Already she had more than enough work. She did not need more. She would simply refuse to do the mentoring. If they ever did speak to her about it, she would pull no punches. They would learn that they had only themselves to blame. She would show them how poorly they had treated a teacher who was willing to help.

At times, when she was calmer, Anne recognized that something was wrong with this. The anger she felt seemed out of proportion to the issue. Still, it was hard to resist the angry thoughts, and they returned periodically as the days passed.

∞

Two days later, in the evening:

"Anne, how are things with you?" Mark asked. "Are you all right?"

"Why do you ask?" Anne replied.

"Well, you've seemed a little on edge recently. Is something bothering you?"

"My turn to say, 'You don't miss much!'" Anne said. She smiled briefly and sat facing Mark. "Yes, something is bothering me. You remember that we talked about the mentoring and agreed that I would accept the offer. I did. I told the principal about this after we spoke. I mentioned to you a week later that I hadn't heard from her. Now it's been more than two weeks, and she still hasn't gotten back to me. It's been weighing on me, and I'm getting frustrated."

"Frustrated?"

"Well, maybe 'angry' is a better word. To be honest, I'm getting quite angry about it. They asked my help. I agreed, and now they don't have the simple courtesy to reply one way or the other."

"Have you been thinking about this a lot?"

"Yes, and the more I do, the angrier I get. I'm considering just telling them that I won't do it. If they are so indifferent about it, why should I put myself out?"

"Anne," Mark said, "I understand that they could communicate better about this. But it is only a few weeks since you spoke with the principal. She may have other people to contact before she can speak definitively with you. Maybe that's why she hasn't gotten back to you yet. And I understand your frustration, but why is it so intense? Why does it bother you so much? And I think this matters: Do you really want to close the door to something that you love and do well simply because no one has said anything in these past weeks?"

"You have a point," Anne said slowly. "I haven't asked myself why this bothers me so much. I probably should. And now that you ask, no, I don't want to close this door."

"I think," Mark said, "that it would be good to pray about this. I'll pray with you. If you reflect more on this and want to talk again, I'll be happy to." ·

"That sounds right," Anne said. "Thank you for noticing and talking about it. That helps. Give me a little time, and then we can talk again."

∞

Over the next days, Anne did pray and reflect about this. Before long, she was able to identify her anger as belonging to a pattern she had noted before in herself. Growing up, the demands of her father's work and her mother's frequent illnesses had left Anne largely on her own. In most matters, she had had to manage for herself. She had learned that "If I don't make it happen, no one else will." This sense was deeply ingrained in her. A sadness and an anger, both of which could be strong, accompanied this awareness. In later life, whenever she felt that others were not present, not doing their part, were ignoring her, or would not help as she needed, that sense of "If I don't make it happen, no one else will," with its attendant sadness and anger surfaced. At such times, she grew angrier than the situation merited. She knew this anger could be destructive.

Anne now saw this pattern in her present anger. She could imagine various reasons why the principal had not yet communicated with her. As Mark had said, the principal might need to consult others, perhaps the finance board and the other teachers. She might be seeking a consensus, and that could take time. Perhaps the new teachers had scheduling issues, and it might be difficult to find a time that worked for all. Further, Anne knew the goodwill and competence of the principal. She was not one to act carelessly or irresponsibly. Whatever the reason for the delay, Anne knew that her cold, angry feelings were not of God and were to be resisted. She resolved, as best she could, to wait in openness for further word about the mentoring.

Anne also planned to review this insight with Mark. She knew that his listening and their conversation would help her better understand this pattern in herself. If she did, her present experience might also help forestall any harm it might cause in the future.

∞

In his final rule, Ignatius again presents a metaphor and its application. First, the metaphor:

> Likewise he [the enemy] conducts himself as a leader, intent upon conquering and robbing what he desires. For, just as a captain and leader of an army in the field, pitching his camp and exploring the fortifications and defenses of a stronghold, attacks it at the weakest point.

The leader of this group of thieves studies the stronghold, identifies the weakest point in the defenses, and attacks it precisely at that point.

Discernment of Spirits in Marriage

Now the application:

> ... in the same way the enemy of human nature, roving about, looks in turn at all our theological, cardinal, and moral virtues; and where he finds us weakest and most in need for our eternal salvation, there he attacks us and attempts to take us.

The enemy, as it were, studies the whole of our spiritual fortress: our prayer; our relationships in marriage, in the family, in the Church, and at work; our activity; what gives us energy and hope; what troubles and disheartens us, and all the rest. He sees where we are weakest, least prepared to defend against him, and precisely there he attacks us.

We all have some point in which we are most vulnerable to the enemy's attack. There is no shame in this! Once more, this is simply what it means to live the spiritual life in a fallen, redeemed, and loved world. From our family, upbringing, experiences in life, temperament, health, relationships—from all that forms who we are—arises a point in which we are most vulnerable: most easily discouraged, saddened, made anxious, angry, impatient, frustrated, inclined to give up prayer, settle for less, heed temptation, and the like. This is the point, Ignatius says, where the enemy will most readily attack us.

If such is the enemy's tactic, what should be our response? Our best defense is to *know* that point and to *strengthen* it, so that the vulnerable point becomes increasingly less vulnerable. If we do this, wonderful consequences follow. The point that discouraged us most often and most deeply is transformed into our most fruitful space of growth.

Through prayer, reflection, and conversation with Mark, Anne identifies what may well be her most vulnerable point: that place of sadness and anger rooted in a limitation of her family of origin. Perceiving this clearly and employing the tools to strengthen this point, she will grow less exposed to an anger that might harm her and her married vocation.

Where might you be most vulnerable to the enemy's attacks? Do you find yourself saying, for example, "I always wind up in this discouraging situation"? Or, "This pattern just keeps repeating, and it always saps my energy for prayer, my marriage, and my family life"? Or, "In this area especially, I feel helpless, and it weighs on me"? If you note a repeating pattern of this kind, then you are well positioned *to strengthen the weak point*. Your married life will change in blessed ways as you seek growth in this specific area.

The enemy will tell you that in this area especially, you will never change. Do not believe it! God's word (Matt. 7:7; Phil. 4:13) and the experience of many prove the contrary.

Identify the most vulnerable point. Use the spiritual means to strengthen it: the sacraments, spiritual direction if possible, the examination of conscience (examen prayer), daily meditative prayer, and spiritual reading on the topic. In addition, use any appropriate human means. Might a few meetings with a professionally competent Catholic counselor help? Anne, for example, might find this so: a deeper understanding of the familial origins of her anger, gained with the help of a counselor, might help her make good choices in its regard.

If Anne can identify her most vulnerable point, and if she works to strengthen it, many blessings will follow. She is a rich human being who loves the Lord. Set free from this vulnerability, her life as a woman, wife, mother, and teacher will grow increasingly happier and more fruitful.

Discernment of Spirits in Marriage

It almost seems that Ignatius saves the best for last. That one area where we find it hard to hope, that seems too strong to overcome, in which we feel condemned to fail—Ignatius will not end his rules without offering hope *right there*. In a deep way, rule 14 shows captives the way to freedom.

A Final Word

It was another fall day. Again the sun shone through the multicolored foliage of the trees that surrounded them. Mark and Anne sat on a park bench, looking at the lake before them.

"Do you remember," Mark said, "that day five years ago when we sat on this same bench? When I told you about the earlier years in my life?"

"You know that I will never forget it."

"Nor will I. Your response that day has shaped everything in my life since. I'll never be able to thank you enough."

Anne laid her hand on his. "I'll never be able to thank God enough for you, for that day, and for all that has happened in our lives since."

"Things do change, don't they," Mark said, "when we begin to understand our experience. You, first of all, and then Father Reed, have made the difference for me."

"Well," Anne replied, "I suppose we should say that God, first of all, has helped us both."

"Yes," Mark said. "So much goes on in our hearts and thoughts. Just beginning to understand what is of God and not of God in it all makes a big difference. Father Reed always speaks of captives set free, and that's a good image."

"Free?" Anne asked.

Mark smiled. "You know what I mean."

Anne, too, smiled. "Yes, but I'd like to hear you say it."

"Free from discouragement, from the lies of the enemy, from that sense of helplessness, from that feeling that things will never change. I lived that way for so long. I still struggle with it at times, but it's less frequent and less oppressive. Most often now, I catch it sooner than in the past. And then, free to love you, to be the husband that you want me to be, to be the father that our children need, to be faithful to God in my work, and to share in the life of the Church."

Anne did not reply immediately. Mark looked at her and saw that she was deeply moved.

"Thank you," she said quietly.

∽

That freedom is the gift of Ignatius's rules (see Luke 4:18). Ignatius tells us that these are "rules for becoming aware and understanding to some extent the different movements that are caused in the soul, the good, to receive them, and the bad to reject them."

These are rules for:

• *Becoming aware*: like Mark and Anne, able to notice the spiritual stirrings in our hearts and thoughts.

• *Understanding*: again, like Mark and Anne, able, in these interior stirrings, to distinguish the discouraging lies of the enemy from the encouraging promptings of the good spirit.

• *Taking action*: joyfully *accepting* the warm, hope-filled promptings of the good spirit, so that we progress solidly toward God, and firmly *rejecting* the discouraging lies of the enemy, so that they never harm us. Mark and Anne are advancing solidly on this blessed journey.

In short:

• Be aware.

• Understand.

• Take action (accept/reject).

To live this way daily is to live the discerning life. When we do, we will experience what Mark and Anne, and countless men and women before them, have experienced: we will be set free to love the Lord, to be the spouses that God calls us to be. May that freedom bless you every day of your married life.

Resources

My purpose in this book is to introduce Ignatius's fourteen rules, specifically as applied to the married vocation. Obviously, much more may be said about them! Here I provide resources for a deeper understanding of them. I can promise you this: if you learn more about these rules, you will be glad, for the rest of your life, that you did.

Books

I have written two full-length books on these rules. The first is more systematic. The second explores additional aspects of the rules and is also more personal. Either book may be read first. The other book, if also read, will reinforce and complete the teaching.

The Discernment of Spirits: An Ignatian Guide to Everyday Living (New York: Crossroad, 2005)

Setting Captives Free: Personal Reflections on Ignatian Discernment of Spirits (New York: Crossroad, 2018)

Discernment of Spirits in Marriage

A guide for individual or group study accompanies the first book:

A *Reader's Guide to The Discernment of Spirits: An Ignatian Guide to Everyday Living* (New York: Crossroad, 2013)

Podcasts

These are fifteen half-hour conversations in which I discuss each rule in detail. The podcasts are free and accessible in the following places:

- discerninghearts.com
- Discerning Hearts App
- YouTube
- iTunes
- Google Play
- FORMED

DVD

I presented this material as a televised series in ten forty-five minute episodes. The DVD is titled *Living the Discerning Life* and is available through the EWTN catalogue and my website:

www.frtimothygallagher.org

The Text of the Fourteen Rules: Original Language

*I call this version the "Original Language" in the sense that my trans-
lation of Ignatius's Spanish text follows that text as closely as English
permits. It is, with few exceptions, almost a transliteration from the
Spanish. The occasional awkwardness of the translation reflects Ignatius's style: rich in content and less concerned about literary niceties.
The translation permits, as much as a translation can, access to the
original both in content and style.*

Saint Ignatius's Fourteen Rules

Rules for becoming aware and understanding to some
extent the different movements that are caused in the
soul—the good, to receive them, and the bad to reject
them.

∞

First rule. The first rule: in persons who are going from
mortal sin to mortal sin, the enemy is ordinarily accustomed to propose apparent pleasures to them, leading

them to imagine sensual delights and pleasures in order to hold them more and make them grow in their vices and sins. In these persons the good spirit uses a contrary method, stinging and biting their consciences through their rational power of moral judgment.

∞

Second rule. The second: in persons who are going on intensely purifying their sins and rising from good to better in the service of God our Lord, the method is contrary to that in the first rule. For then it is proper to the evil spirit to bite, sadden, and place obstacles, disquieting with false reasons, so that the person may not go forward. And it is proper to the good spirit to give courage and strength, consolations, tears, inspirations, and quiet, easing and taking away all obstacles, so that the person may go forward in doing good.

∞

Third rule. The third is of spiritual consolation. I call it consolation when some interior movement is caused in the soul, through which the soul comes to be inflamed with love of its Creator and Lord, and, consequently when it can love no created thing on the face of the earth in itself, but only in the Creator of them all. Likewise when it sheds tears that move to love of its Lord, whether out of sorrow for one's sins, or for the passion of Christ our Lord, or because of other things directly ordered to his service and praise. Finally, I call consolation every increase of hope, faith, and charity, and all interior joy that calls and attracts to heavenly things and to the salvation of one's soul, quieting it and giving it peace in its Creator and Lord.

∞

Fourth rule. The fourth is of spiritual desolation. I call desolation all the contrary of the third rule, such as darkness of soul, disturbance in it, movement to low and earthly things, disquiet from various agitations and temptations, moving to lack of confidence, without hope, without love, finding oneself totally slothful, tepid, sad, and as if separated from one's Creator and Lord. For just as consolation is contrary to desolation, in the same way the thoughts that come from consolation are contrary to the thoughts that come from desolation.

∞

Fifth rule. The fifth: in time of desolation never make a change, but be firm and constant in the proposals and determination in which one was the day preceding such desolation, or in the determination in which one was in the preceding consolation. Because, as in consolation the good spirit guides and counsels us more, so in desolation the bad spirit, with whose counsels we cannot find the way to a right decision.

∞

Sixth rule. The sixth: although in desolation we should not change our first proposals, it is very advantageous to change ourselves intensely against the desolation itself, as by insisting more upon prayer, meditation, upon much examination, and upon extending ourselves in some suitable way of doing penance.

∞

Seventh rule. The seventh: let one who is in desolation consider how the Lord has left him in trial in his natural powers, so that he may resist the various agitations and temptations of the enemy; since he can resist with the divine help, which always remains with him, though he does not clearly feel it; for the Lord has taken away from him his great fervor, abundant love, and intense grace, leaving him, however, sufficient grace for eternal salvation.

∞

Eighth rule. The eighth: let one who is in desolation work to be in patience, which is contrary to the vexations which come to him, and let him think that he will soon be consoled, diligently using the means against such desolation, as is said in the sixth rule.

∞

Ninth rule. The ninth: there are three principal causes for which we find ourselves desolate. The first is because we are tepid, slothful, or negligent in our spiritual exercises, and so through our faults spiritual consolation withdraws from us. The second, to try us and see how much we are and how much we extend ourselves in his service and praise without so much payment of consolations and increased graces. The third, to give us true recognition and understanding so that we may interiorly feel that it is not ours to attain or maintain increased devotion, intense love, tears, or any other spiritual consolation, but that all is the gift and grace of God our Lord, and so that we may not build a nest in something belonging to another, raising our mind in some pride or vainglory, attributing to ourselves the devotion or the other parts of the spiritual consolation.

∞

Tenth rule. The tenth: let the one who is in consolation think how he will conduct himself in the desolation which will come after, taking new strength for that time.

∞

Eleventh rule. The eleventh: let one who is consoled seek to humble himself and lower himself as much as he can, thinking of how little he is capable in the time of desolation without such grace or consolation. On the contrary, let one who is in desolation think that he can do much with God's sufficient grace to resist all his enemies, taking strength in his Creator and Lord.

∞

Twelfth rule. The twelfth: the enemy acts as spoiled children do in being weak when faced with strength and strong when faced with weakness. For it is proper to spoiled children, when they begin to act out, to lose heart and desist when their parents confront them firmly; and, on the contrary, if their parents respond with weakness and helplessness, their acting out grows greatly and knows no bounds. In the same way, it is proper to the enemy to weaken and lose heart, fleeing and ceasing his temptations when the person who is exercising himself in spiritual things confronts the temptations of the enemy firmly, doing what is diametrically opposed to them; and, on the contrary, if the person who is exercising himself begins to be afraid and lose heart in suffering the temptations, there is no beast so fierce on the face of the earth as the enemy of human nature in following out his damnable intention with such growing malice.

∞

Thirteenth rule. The thirteenth: likewise he conducts himself as a false lover in wishing to remain secret and not be revealed. For a dissolute man who, speaking with evil intention, makes dishonorable advances to a daughter of a good father or a wife of a good husband, wishes his words and persuasions to be secret, and the contrary displeases him very much, when the daughter reveals to her father or the wife to her husband his false words and depraved intention, because he easily perceives that he will not be able to succeed with the undertaking begun. In the same way, when the enemy of human nature brings his wiles and persuasions to the just soul, he wishes and desires that they be received and kept in secret; but when one reveals them to one's good confessor or to another spiritual person, who knows his deceits and malicious designs, it weighs on him very much, because he perceives that he will not be able to succeed with the malicious undertaking he has begun, since his manifest deceits have been revealed.

∞

Fourteenth rule. The fourteenth: likewise he conducts himself as a leader, intent upon conquering and robbing what he desires. For, just as a captain and leader of an army in the field, pitching his camp and exploring the fortifications and defenses of a stronghold, attacks it at the weakest point, in the same way the enemy of human nature, roving about, looks in turn at all our theological, cardinal and moral virtues; and where he finds us weakest and most in need for our eternal salvation, there he attacks us and attempts to take us.

The Text of the Fourteen Rules: Contemporary Version

First rule. When a person lives a life of serious sin, the enemy fills the imagination with images of sensual pleasures; the good spirit stings and bites in the person's conscience, God's loving action, calling the person back.

∞

Second rule. When a person tries to avoid sin and to love God, this reverses: now the enemy tries to bite, discourage, and sadden; the good spirit gives courage, strength, and inspirations, easing the path forward.

∞

Third rule. When your heart finds joy in God, a sense of God's closeness and love, you are experiencing spiritual consolation. Open your heart to God's gift!

∞

Fourth rule. When your heart is discouraged, you have little energy for spiritual things, and God feels far away, you are experiencing spiritual desolation. Resist and reject this tactic of the enemy!

∞

Fifth rule. In time of desolation, never make a change! When you are in spiritual desolation, never change anything in your spiritual life.

∞

Sixth rule. When you are in spiritual desolation, use these four means: prayer (ask God's help!), meditation (think of Bible verses, truths about God's faithful love, memories of God's fidelity to you in the past), examination (ask: What am I feeling? How did this start?), and suitable penance (don't just give in and don't immerse yourself in social media, music, movies, and so forth). Stand your ground in suitable ways!

∞

Seventh rule. When you are in spiritual desolation, *think* of this truth: God is giving me all the grace I need to get safely through this desolation.

∞

Eighth rule. When you are in spiritual desolation, be patient, stay the course, and remember that consolation will return much sooner than the desolation is telling you.

∞

Ninth rule. Why does a God who loves us allow us to experience spiritual desolation? To help us see changes we need to make, to strengthen us in our resistance to desolation, and to help us not to become complacent in the spiritual life.

∞

Tenth rule. When you are in spiritual consolation, remember that desolation will return at some point, and prepare for it.

∞

Eleventh rule. The mature person of discernment is neither carelessly high in consolation nor despairingly low in desolation, but humble in consolation and trusting in desolation.

∞

Twelfth rule. Resist the enemy's temptations right at their very beginning. This is when it is easiest.

∞

Thirteenth rule. When you find burdens on your heart in your spiritual life, temptations, confusion, discouragement, find a wise, competent spiritual person, and talk about it.

∞

Fourteenth rule. Identify that area of your life where you are most vulnerable to the enemy's temptations and discouraging lies, and strengthen it.

About the Author

Father Timothy M. Gallagher, OMV, was ordained in 1979 as a member of the Oblates of the Virgin Mary, a religious community dedicated to giving retreats and spiritual formation according to the Spiritual Exercises of Saint Ignatius. Having obtained his doctorate in 1983 from the Gregorian University, he has taught (Saint John's Seminary, Brighton, Massachusetts; Our Lady of Grace Seminary Residence, Boston), assisted in formation work, and served two terms as provincial in his community. He is a frequent speaker on EWTN, and his digitally recorded talks are used around the world. He has written ten books on Ignatian discernment and prayer and several books on Venerable Bruno Lanteri and the Liturgy of the Hours. He currently holds the Saint Ignatius Chair for Spiritual Formation at Saint John Vianney Theological Seminary in Denver.

Sophia Institute

Sophia Institute is a nonprofit institution that seeks to nurture the spiritual, moral, and cultural life of souls and to spread the Gospel of Christ in conformity with the authentic teachings of the Roman Catholic Church.

Sophia Institute Press fulfills this mission by offering translations, reprints, and new publications that afford readers a rich source of the enduring wisdom of mankind.

Sophia Institute also operates the popular online resource CatholicExchange.com. *Catholic Exchange* provides world news from a Catholic perspective as well as daily devotionals and articles that will help readers to grow in holiness and live a life consistent with the teachings of the Church.

In 2013, Sophia Institute launched Sophia Institute for Teachers to renew and rebuild Catholic culture through service to Catholic education. With the goal of nurturing the spiritual, moral, and cultural life of souls, and an abiding respect for the role and work of teachers, we strive to provide materials and programs that are at once enlightening to the mind and ennobling to the heart; faithful and complete, as well as useful and practical.

Sophia Institute gratefully recognizes the Solidarity Association for preserving and encouraging the growth of our apostolate over the course of many years. Without their generous and timely support, this book would not be in your hands.

www.SophiaInstitute.com
www.CatholicExchange.com
www.SophiaInstituteforTeachers.org

Sophia Institute Press® is a registered trademark of Sophia Institute.
Sophia Institute is a tax-exempt institution as defined by the
Internal Revenue Code, Section 501(c)(3). Tax ID 22-2548708.